To Jim & Lisa,
Beer is culture!
Cheers, [signature] 10·11·14

COOL BEER LABELS

THE BEST ART & DESIGN FROM BREWERIES AROUND THE WORLD

DANIEL BELLON & STEVEN SPEEG

Things that make Jim + Lisa "Cool"
1. guitar master work.
2. lover cool design
3. Super Awesome

Cheers
— Steven Speeg

PRINT
Cincinnati, Ohio
www.printmag.com

For more excellent books and resources for designers, visit www.printmag.com.

18 17 16 15 14   5 4 3 2 1

ISBN-13: 978-1-4403-3520-4

Distributed in Canada by Fraser Direct
100 Armstrong Avenue
Georgetown, Ontario, Canada L7G 5S4
Tel: (905) 877-4411

Distributed in the U.K. and Europe by F&W Media International, LTD
Brunel House, Forde Close, Newton Abbot, TQ12 4PU, UK
Tel: (+44) 1626 323200, Fax: (+44) 1626 323319
Email: enquiries@fwmedia.com

Distributed in Australia by Capricorn Link
P.O. Box 704, Windsor, NSW 2756 Australia
Tel: (02) 4560-1600

Edited by Scott Francis
Art Directed by Claudean Wheeler
Designed by Daniel Bellon
Cover photograph by Klaus Bellon
Production coordinated by Greg Nock

a content + ecommerce company

Dan's Acknowledgments

A lot of people contributed to making this book happen, so trying to thank everyone is a futile endeavor. I just hope none of the people omitted will take it personally and want to kick my ass next time I see them.

First, I should thank Steve Speeg. Not that there was any doubt, but we made a great team and saw this thing through. Thanks bro.

A huge thanks goes out Claudean Wheeler and Scott Francis at Print Books. They both believed in this book, even before I did. Your names should be on the cover of this book, along with ours. Well, maybe not.

Cheers to all the breweries, designers, photographers and illustrators that helped out by providing work. This would be a pretty boring, and short book without all your help. Thanks to my brother Klaus for his support, love and all the photography, including the cover. Special thanks to Nickie Peña and, of course, Greg Koch at Stone Brewing. As busy and amazing as you guys are, you took the time to pay attention to a couple of beer nerds with a crazy idea.

Finally, I lovingly thank my wife, Jo, for putting up with the craziness that was my working on this project. Her eternal patience was instrumental to the completion of this book.

Steve's Acknowledgments

I would like to thank Daniel Bellon for asking me to help out on this adventure of a book. You introduced me to some fantastic beers and we have shared many enlightening conversations, but your friendship has been the most valued. You are like a brother to me and I will always have your back.

To my brother, Adam Speeg, for tracking down my first bottle of 120 min IPA, and more importantly, teaching me how to brew my own beer. I love you, man.

To Mark Sigman from Relic Brewing for the cooperation and the inspiration. Your beers have added some much needed refinement to my palate.

To my friends and co-workers: Thank you for listening, offering advice, and supporting me through this entire journey. Extra thanks to ChaChanna Simpson, David Fletcher, Michael Defte Delaporte, Craig Gilbert, Ben Keene, and Bethany Bandera.

Special thanks goes to my always supportive and amazing wife, Kathryn Speeg. She not only provided her photography skills, she also traveled with me to package stores, breweries and beer fests, all with a smile on her face. Thanks for your insight. You have always believed in me and told me that anything is possible. It's you and me against the world. I love you.

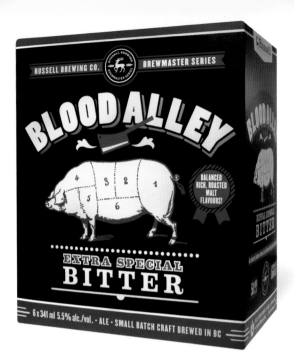

RUSSELL BREWING CO. · BREWMASTER SERIES

BLOOD ALLEY

BALANCED RICH, ROASTED MALT FLAVOURS!

EXTRA SPECIAL BITTER

6 x 341 ml 5.5% alc./vol. · ALE · SMALL BATCH CRAFT BREWED IN BC

Russell Brewing Company
Surrey, British Columbia, Canada
RussellBeer.com

Design by Atmosphere Design
Vancouver, British Columbia, Canada
AtmosphereDesign.ca

Contents

Foreword

by Greg Koch, CEO & Co-founder, Stone Brewing Co.

I love beer. No, not like your buddy who polishes off a 24-pack every weekend. That's a love of drinking. I mean I love beer. Real beer. And not just the beer itself... I'm passionate about the idea of beer. Great beer represents a vast number of things—passion, artistry, authenticity, creativity and honesty. It's all of this that fuels my fanaticism.

I'm known for sometimes talking in terms evocative of a revolutionary who's joined the collective call for "Freedom!" and there's a reason for that: I've joined the collective call for freedom of access to great beer. In fact, many consider me a zealot. It was my zealotry that led me to start Stone Brewing Co. with my business partner (and more importantly, our brewmaster), Steve Wagner, in 1996.

In the years prior, I'd become fascinated by the art, integrity and inventiveness of small brewers. However, my journey down the rabbit hole of great beer actually took several years. Such was the reality of living in Los Angeles in the craft-beer-starved, pre-Internet days of the late 1980s and early 1990s. Back then, the call to action for better, higher quality beer came from only a small group, but it was a fierce and ardent assemblage. I heard that call, and it resonated with me. Yes, principally because I realized that the words "awesome" and "beer" could actually coexist in the same sentence, but also in part because of my discovery that I'd been lied to when told that all that industrial, fizzy, yellow stuff was beer.

Now I knew better. I was in.

Since then, a lot has changed. The quantity and availability of quality ales and lagers has greatly increased. In today's world, I feel there is no excuse for a bar, restaurant or hotel not to make great choices available to me as a customer. With so much craft beer being produced, and such an undeniable demand for it, it's more of a conscious choice for public venues not to participate, and if an establishment makes that decision, then I'm going to make the same one—I'm going elsewhere. I simply will not tolerate anyone offering me mediocrity when excellence is so frequently available. Period.

While many people still think of beer as the industrialized facsimile stuff, that's not beer. At least not to me. Nor should it be to anyone else. While we once had to settle, as a nation, we have broken free from the chains of low expectations, from the insulting insinuation by large corporations that we don't want or deserve better. At Stone, our focus has always been on providing something better, and we are proud to be part of an industry that shares that altruistic objective.

Nothing represents this new age in beer or the true passion and artistry of this industry like the beer label. Ironically, nothing represents the dark side better, either. Fortunately, this book focuses on the former. But allow me to digress, all the same. After all, having whetted your appetite for scandal, I'm sure you want to know my thoughts on the latter.

I'm not going to name names, but I will call out the dark side of the beer label: Lies. I'm one to draw hard lines. I see little difference between a company knowingly allowing the public to believe something that's not true, often designing packaging and slogans that are specifically aimed at that goal... and a company based on outright mistruths. All are intended to allow us to believe something that's not true.

Case in point: a label that suggests a beer is made somewhere it's not. Or by a company it's not. Or on an island it's not. Or in an area code where it's not. By a small, independent company, when it's not. By a small brewery that doesn't actually exist except on a paper label. That's horseshit! I believe the truth should be easy to understand and require no special knowledge to flush out.

Of course, those negatives, funnily enough, highlight what's great about beer labels, too. They can be pieces of art that convey far more than technical information. They are capable of conveying style, often a sense of place, an attitude, or a philosophy. I know beer labels that are nods to comic art, to death metal music and to mythology. And that's just from one brewery!

When it came time to create the labels for Stone, it was a laborious process. Looking back, the choices seem obvious, but at the time, it was painful. The main challenge was finding the right artist to help me create my vision. A

Stone Brewing Co.
Escondido, California
StoneBrewing.com
Design by Stone Brewing Co.

big part of it was that I wasn't 100% sure just what that vision was. Minor detail. I had a variety of artists, all extremely talented, submit ideas that were so far off the mark I'd wonder if they'd heard a single word I'd said. Finally, after seeing some fantastic fantasy art at a local t-shirt screen printing shop, I asked for the name of the artist. Fortuitously, it was a local guy named Tom Matthews, and I was able to get his contact info.

Tom was intrigued with the idea of creating an iconic gargoyle figure that would convey the weightiness of a time-worn guardian, the fierceness of a protector who wouldn't hesitate to leap to the defense of dearly held ideals, and the air of superior knowledge and taste embodied in his visage. It was a tall order, but Tom was up to it.

It was a birthing process. The number of iterations were voluminous, and Tom was intrepid in putting up with my constant feedback, which ranged from outright rejections to a steady flow of tweaks. But the results were worth the process and, in the end, we developed a character that clearly communicated, "I stand for something, and DO NOT try to get me to settle for less. Ever."

I often joke that while Tom drew the gargoyle and I created the rest of the label, I can point to the rectangular square in which the gargoyle and text rested and the small squares creating very modest flourishes in the corners, and say, "Yep. I drew that." A large rectangle and some small squares—my, what talent I possess! But the truth was that the gargoyle didn't need anything other than a simple frame within which to rest

les, I created the font work as well (to the degree that you can call selecting the Castellar font "creating"), and arranged the overall layout of the original labels.

Since that time, all label artwork has come from within Stone. Originally me, then for many years, Mike Palmer (Mike has worked with Stone since the very beginning, and continues with us to this day as our art department's Creative Director), and in recent years, a small but formidable team of talented in-house artists. The only exception has been the gargoyles themselves, which have all come from two local artists—first, Tom Matthews and later, Edson Ruiz (who drew what we now know as the "Anniversary Gargoyle," the "Bistro Gargoyle" and the "Sublimely Self-Righteous Gargoyle").

Additionally, I believe we were the first brewery to use the opportunity afforded by the label's back panel to write more than a few sentences of text. Like many, I grew up reading the backs of cereal boxes. I wanted to convey our principles, philosophies and ideals to people, and since we didn't have any marketing budget at Stone, I used the only platform that was available to me. And it took. Nowadays, it's common to see a host of writing on the back labels of beer bottles. Some of our labels have themes... Arrogant Bastard Ale, OAKED Arrogant Bastard Ale and Double Bastard Ale most certainly do, with their diatribes railing against mediocrity and mindless mass-consumerism.

So does Stone Old Guardian Barley Wine, which comes out in the first quarter of each year. Over the last ten years or so, I've developed a ritual

of writing the annual prose for the upcoming edition of that beer around late November whilst enjoying a bottle of the current vintage as my muse. Written in a stream-of-consciousness style, I reflect on the previous year, the upcoming year, and details about where I am and what I'm doing at the moment. I'm pretty sure that Stone Old Guardian Barley Wine has the most words on it of any beer label in history. What I'm not sure about is that this is something for which I should feel a sense of pride. Nonetheless, I do. I have a feeling that probably the vast majority of people don't read it, which is perfectly fine, but it's there, should you feel inclined. I have a theory that if you start reading the bottle after you've taken your first sip of the beer, you don't stand a chance of finishing the label. The challenge of finishing the over-12% ABV barley wine is significant enough. Thus, if you'd like to finish both, I recommend reading at least the first few lines before your first sip.

No matter how many quality craft beers you indulge in during your perusal of this tome devoted to the almighty power of the beer label, make sure you get all the way to the end. Your thoroughness is sure to be rewarded with a better understanding of the artistic nature of this often overlooked medium, as well as an enhanced thirst for something real and something better.

Cheers,

Greg Koch,
CEO & Co-founder, Stone Brewing Co.

A Book About Beer Labels

by Daniel Bellon

After my last book, *Typography for the People*, was released in 2010, I thought, "Never again." A book is a lot of work. A book is too much work. It's more than I ever imagined before working on one. However, just like a night when you drank too much, it is all worth it when you look back. At first the hangover gets the best of you, but that passes and soon enough, you forget all about what you promised yourself. Never again? Well, here I am, once again, with a cool one in front of me.

So, why do it again, then? Close the book you're holding right now (bookmark the page, of course), read the cover and you'll know why I decided to do it again: beer and design—two of my biggest passions combined. This is not the type of project you take on for money or fame. You do it because it's simply awesome. You do it because if you don't do it, someone else will, and your chance to sell and sign copies of your book at small beer festivals all over the world will go to someone else. The process, though, was a little more complicated than that short, beer-and-design answer.

Why You Should Always Listen to Your Father

The story of this book begins years ago. Like most us, I grew up drinking terrible beer. I have no excuse, though. My father was German. I always knew he drank "fancy" German beer, but I never cared enough to even ask him why. If I would have just asked then, I could have spared myself years of drinking horrible, tasteless beer, but I was young and foolish and threw away the opportunity to learn about good beer at an early age. Once I was old enough to actually start drinking beer, price and availability—not quality—were the paramount factors behind my choice. So I went to the supermarket and bought whatever was on sale.

In 1997, during my days as an obnoxious front man in a loud punk rock band, I got the opportunity to tour Europe for three weeks. The band didn't play in arenas in front of thousands; we played small bars in front of hundreds. We didn't make millions; we got paid enough for gas money and very often not even that. Our tour manager, a friendly, tall, skinny German named Uli, started suggesting paying us in beer to those who couldn't afford to pay after the concerts. All our expenses were taken care of by the record label, so we were, in essence, driving around in Europe for free and now we had cases of beer to enjoy. One thing became apparent right away: Some of this beer didn't taste like dirty water. It had flavor, body and aroma. It wasn't the type of beer you just wanted to chug. You could actually taste it. Furthermore, as we went from Spain to France, onto Germany, Poland and the Czech Republic, the beers tasted different. I'm not going to tell you that

every beer we had was a superb, extra-tasty, dark lager brewed to perfection. Thinking back I am sure most of what we had was probably quite terrible, but for my uninitiated tongue the mere idea that different beers could taste different was a revelation.

Another surprise came when we were in a small town in Poland and the bartender at the place we were playing at that night told me he actually made the beer they sold there. People make beer? I knew people made pie and cookies, and I'd even heard of crazy people making their own wine, but people make beer? That trip to Europe changed the way I looked at and tasted beer. When I got back home I sat with my dad and enjoyed a Dunkel German lager.

Unlike beer, I have been interested in good design and typography since an early age. My father, an engineer, also had an infatuation with design. Unlike my dismissal of his taste in beer, his knowledge of design intrigued me. I grew up surrounded by books and framed prints of work by Raymond Loewy, Ferdinand Porsche, and later Paul Rand and László Moholy-Nagy. I went on to study graphic design at the University of Cincinnati, where I truly fell in love with the craft, especially with typography. It wasn't until I seriously became interested in beer that I realized that there was a definite link between the two worlds. Some breweries want to differentiate themselves from big commercial breweries, and good packaging is a great way to do that. Different packaging evokes a feeling of revolution that a lot of small breweries have. It's not an overcommercialized, slick design for the masses; it's niche design for the few. This rebel attitude of some breweries and homebrewers calls for a certain aesthetic, a way to stand apart from supermarket beers in concept and audience. Of course, not every small brewery has well designed packaging, just as not every designer out there loves beer, but you are holding 208 pages that affirm the fact that there is a strong link between the two.

Becoming a Book

My good friend Claudean Wheeler, who has more or less become my literary agent, poked me again to think of another book idea, just as she had done many years ago for *Typography for the People*. "I don't think I have another one in me," I lied. I just didn't want to deal with the whole book thing again. "Think about a few ideas and let me know," she said. So, I did what any self-respecting published author would—nothing. Weeks went by and I got another email: "Did you think of any ideas?" "Of course!" Another lie.

I had to think fast. What are the few things I like so much I won't mind spending the next

SkullKrusher Robot Series
Brewed and Designed by Daniel Bellon

two years of my life thinking about? I like pancakes, heavy metal, pizza, professional cycling, tattoos, Mexican wrestling, racecars and beer. I answered the email quickly including a few ideas with the aforementioned awesome topics. The two that I thought had the most legs were a book about the passion of wrestling fans in Mexico and a silly idea to photograph cool looking beer bottles and make a book out of them.

I was excited about the beer idea, but I wasn't sure if anything would really come of it. Little did I know that there was a variable I had not considered: a variable named Scott Francis. Scott is an awesome, and very smart editor at HOW + PRINT Books. (I just said all that, since I know he'll be reading this more than a few times.) Scott is a fellow beer lover and believed in the idea from the beginning. I'll spare you the details of the negotiations, but I'll just tell you there was a meeting in a private jet, a brawl at a seedy bar in Covington, Kentucky, and a few duffel bags of cash exchanging hands. I lie. Simply put: Scott worked his magic with the people upstairs, and they agreed. The book, they said, would have an audience.

The project was green-lighted and I started doing some research. Very early in the research process (within the first hour), I realized there was no way I was going to be able to do this alone. I needed a coauthor.

The first and only name that came to mind was Steven Speeg. We had met at work in Connecticut a few years back and became good friends. Steve was the first homebrewer I ever met and he knew beer. I loved craft beer by then, but Steve was a real Beer Guy. He taught me a lot about the world of beer geekdom, but more importantly, he gave me the home brewing bug. He was there the first few times I brewed at home and he was my go-to guy when I needed to tell someone how great (or horrible) the beer I just had was. Steve also happens to be an amazing designer, art director and a very well-organized individual. I got him on the phone and he was on board within minutes. Shortly before we hung up he thanked me for thinking of him. "Oh, you won't be so thankful in a few months when we are up to our ears in work," I thought. He didn't know it at the time, but it was I who should have been thanking him.

The Title

Cool
We've been asked hundreds of times how we chose the beers to be featured. What does the "cool" in *Cool Beer Labels* mean? Well, some of the labels and cans are very well designed, some have great typography, and some are nice illustrations. Some are odd and quirky; others may seem plain but have a really nice, elegant look. We didn't want to make this book a showcase of snobby excellence in graphic design and typography. We consciously chose to ignore the little designer voices in our heads. The truth is that we didn't have a set of rules that the beers had to measure up to. It was all gut. It was all "Wow, that beer looks cool!" When I first started working on the book, I really thought it was going to be difficult to come up with enough material to fill 200-plus pages, but as the months went by, the opposite became apparent. There's a lot of cool beer packaging out there. We are crossing our fingers for the chance to do a second book.

Beer
I like beer. Beer makes me happy. What is it about beer that makes some of us like it so much? By some estimates beer has been around for more than 10,000 years. People have been making beer for as long as they've been planting grain, many thousands of years before the wheel was invented. So, it has been around for a long, long, long time, but why is beer so appealing? I believe there are two reasons: taste and people. I love tasting different beers and there's a whole world of taste possibilities. (I'd be doing the world a disservice if I didn't try them all!) Then there's the beer community. From the guy you meet at the bar, to the brewers you meet at a beer festival, we all have something in common. Like any subculture, I guess, beer brings people together and gives us something to talk about.

Labels
We use the term "labels" very loosely. The book features much more than labels, but *Cool Beer Packaging, Including Labels on Bottles, Screened Bottles, Cans, Growlers and Other Containers* seemed like too long of a title.

So here you have it: a book about beer labels. A lot of work has gone into this book, not only from myself and Steve, but also from the folks at PRINT Books and all the breweries, designers, agencies, homebrewers and photographers who have helped out. This book is a celebration of beer, beer culture, design and creativity.

This book is a nod to those of us who think, Hmm ... I've never had this one, but the can looks cool; I'll give it a try. To those people I raise my beer. Cheers! ●

A Beer Geek's Journey

by Steven Speeg

Judge With Me
(Magic Hat Brewing Company: #9)

"Don't judge a book by its cover." That's what everyone says, right? Well, not this guy. Oh, I judge. Stick with me and we can do a lot of judging together.

I have always enjoyed well-designed labels and have found some amazing music and books because their covers drew me in. My first introduction into the world of craft beer was by a magical label. I was at the package store (that's what us New Englanders call the liquor store), grabbing a sixer of my favorite beer when my eye happened on the swirling enchanted label for Magic Hat #9. I swapped out my usual purchase and to my delight the beer inside was different enough to intrigue my twenty-three-year-old taste buds. It had malty apricot notes and a crisp finish. That taste put me on a quest to find new and exciting palate-challenging beers. That quest continues to this day. (Join my adventure on Untappd@spookyspeeg). See? Cover: judged. The beer: great.

Designing
(Bass Brewers Limited: Bass Pale Ale)

Back in 1992, I was a junior in high school who had a love for design. I just did not know exactly what design was. I liked photography, but more than the photography itself, I really enjoyed mounting my photographs. That's where I felt I had the most creative freedom. I would print multiple copies of the same photograph and adjust the developing slightly on each one to get darker variations, then I would cut, tear and rotate the photos, putting them together to make a new image. I loved working with the negative space between the photos and following lines that were in the backgrounds to link them. To explore the possibilities of these ideas, I went on to study graphic design at Paier College of Art in Hamden, Connecticut. There I became fascinated by such bold greats like Josef Albers and Herbert Bayer. I can remember plowing through color theory and typography homework with a Bass Pale Ale in hand, thinking that I found something that I truly enjoy doing and that life was going to be all right.

From Imbibing to Brewing
(Anheuser-Busch InBev: Budweiser)

I wasn't always the craft beer geek that I am today. I actually did not even like the taste of beer until my twenties, and even then it was on shaky terms. Yet, I was always intrigued by the label art. I can remember my father, a tried-and-true Budweiser drinker, asking a young me to grab him a beer from the fridge. The intricate crests and flowing ribbons mesmerized me; they reminded me of the patterns on a dollar bill. I asked him, "What does beer taste like?" He smiled and gave me the can. I took a sip and my mouth was filled with this fizzy yellow bitterness. I immediately proclaimed to my laughing Dad that it was grossest thing I had ever tasted and that I didn't know how he could drink it.

Fast forward to a few years ago when my wife, the brilliant woman that she is, surprised me on Father's Day with a homebrew kit. She did plenty of research and went all out: the kit had everything to get started making my own beer, and she got me every little gadget I would need. So what did I do? Well, first, I read the book that came with it: the wonderful *The Complete Joy of Homebrewing* by the great Charlie Papazian. This book, with its quirky illustrations and repeating mantra of "Relax, have a homebrew," was delightful. And what did I do next? Well, I put the kit in the back of my closet and shut the door. I was intimidated. I had visions of alchemists in dark dungeons with bubbling beakers working in secrecy on strange elixirs. As easy and straightforward as the book and directions were, that kit stayed in the back of my closet for over a year.

Then my older brother, Adam (of Skulls Brew House), called me up to say that he had just

Possession Pale Ale
Brewed and Designed by Steven Speeg

brewed his first batch of homebrew. Wha-what! He brewed his own beer? He told me how simple it was and that he would be happy to assist on my first brew. I had to get ready, so I dug out my brew kit from the back of my closet. I got reacquainted with the process, and as turned out, it was not as tricky as I remembered it. Maybe it was the fact that my brother had actually brewed his own beer that gave that me the perspective I needed, but suddenly, that alchemist in the dungeon started looking like a cool dude with a kick-ass beard hanging out in his backyard making his own beer.

Brew Day
(Dogfish Head: 60 Minute IPA)

The big day arrived. I packed up all the supplies. With a twinkle in my eye and a fresh six-pack of Dogfish Head 60 Minute IPA, I headed over to my brother's house.

As the wort from my Centennial IPA was boiling and awaiting one more hop addition, I realized what a supreme time I was having. My brother and I were bonding and talking in a way that we had never done before. Brewing was bringing us closer. As I left his house with a full carboy of greatness, I knew I was hooked on home brewing. For all you homebrewers out there, you can understand the excitement and good vibes that go along with brewing your own beer. To anyone else who is thinking of jumping into the world of homebrewing: Jump in! Pick up a book, or, better yet, go to your local homebrew shop and tell them you want to get started. Those guys are always helpful and willing to take the time to talk with you.

I woke up the next morning and immediately ran to check on the brew. I saw the rolling fermentation going on inside my carboy, and that's when it hit me: I get to name and design a label for this beer! Quickly my mind started swirling like the mysterious liquid in my carboy. What should I name it? Then the bigger thought hit me: I can name my own brewery! I was creating beer and now I was creating a brand identity too! I have never felt so alive. I need a logo... Stickers are a must... Is 200 business cards enough? How much would it cost to rent that billboard downtown? My worlds were coming together: design and beer. I had a new way to express my art. That was the day Spooky Brewery was born and I named my first batch of beer Dead Eye IPA.

SkullKrusher
(Köstritzer Schwarzbierbrauerei GmbH & Co.: Schwarzbier)

Dan Bellon and I worked together in the same creative department. On his first day, I overheard him speaking to a coworker and immediately thought, "This dude is nuts!" After we met, we realized we both love horror movies, pizza, doom and gloom metal, Cincinnati chili, King Diamond, fantasy art and beer. Needless to say, we hit it off right away.

Dan is one of those unique individuals that can weave a compelling story from the most mundane occurrences by peppering in insults, jokes and sound effects, all while reenacting key moments. (Mundane occurrences, though, are rare because crazy stuff tends to happen around him.) He juggles all this and comes off charming.

When he started talking about homebrewing, I was right there to assist with his inaugural brew. With a six pack of Köstritzer and a Manowar DVD in hand, we ordered a pizza, fired up the stove, cracked open a beer and began to brew. Dan was just as charged as I was my first time brewing: "We are brewing beer!" he said. I replied, "I know; isn't it awesome?" Dan was a natural and picked it up right away. His SkullKrusher Dunkelweizen was a delicious, full-bodied ale that he must brew again.

Brew and Design Together
(Relic Brewing Company: Fortnight IPA)

I knew there was some cool label art on beer around the world, but while doing research for this book I realized that there is a huge amount of frame-worthy art out there. Breweries are not only crafting masterpieces with the ingredients inside their bottles and cans, but they are creating works of art for the outside: from simple and clean typography, to whimsical playful illustrations, to paintings of sun-soaked landscapes. As I sit here sipping on a Fortnight IPA, I am inspired and invigorated. I am eager to start my next homebrew, especially since I have already designed the labels.

Thanks for sharing my journey, and my hope is that this book leaves you just as inspired as I am. Cheers! ●

Drake's Brewing Company
San Leandro, California
DrinkDrakes.com

Design by Molly McCoy
Oakland, California
MollyMcCoy.com

01 The West

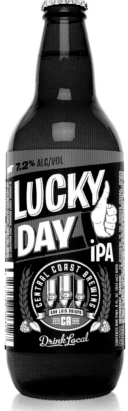

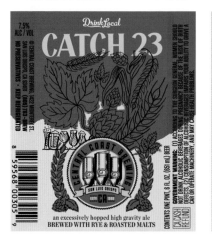

Central Coast Brewing Company
San Luis Obispo, California
CentralCoastBrewing.com

Design by Guru Design (Scott Greci)
Baton Rouge, Louisiana
GuruDesignCo.com

Saint Archer Brewing Company
San Diego, California
SaintArcherBrewery.com

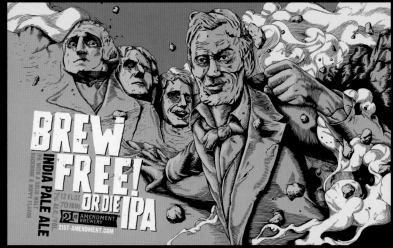

21st Amendment Brewery
San Francisco, California
21st-Amendment.com

Design by TBD Agency
Bend, Oregon
TBDagency.com

Drake's Brewing Company
San Leandro, California
DrinkDrakes.com

Design by Molly McCoy
Oakland, California
MollyMcCoy.com

Crux Fermentation Project
Bend, Oregon
CruxFermentation.com

Design by TBD Agency
Bend, Oregon
TBDagency.com
Photography by Steve Tague & Tyler Rowe

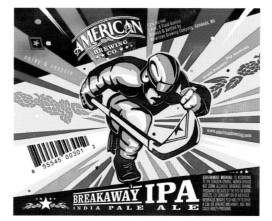

American Brewing Co.
Edmonds, Washington
AmericanBrewing.com

Design by BLINDTIGER Design
Seattle, Washington
BlindtigerDesign.com

Stone Brewing Co.
Escondido, California
StoneBrewing.com
Design by Stone Brewing Co.

Base Camp Brewing Company
Portland, Oregon
BaseCampBrewingCo.com

Design by Base Camp Brewing Company
(Joseph Dallas)

THE WEST

Ninkasi Brewing Company
Eugene, Oregon
NinkasiBrewing.com
Design by Ninkasi (Tony Figoli)

Hopworks Urban Brewery
Portland, Oregon
HopworksBeer.com

Design by Jolby & Friends
Portland, Oregon
JolbyAndFriends.com
Photography by Adam Levey

BLINDTIGER Design
Seattle, Washington

Oceania Eagan, founder of BLINDTIGER Design, was born on Orcas Island, about one hundred miles north of Seattle. Her mother was a designer, so Eagan grew up around commercial art. "From a very early age, I was sitting at the other end of our kitchen table mimicking her. When she was designing a restaurant menu, I was designing a restaurant menu; when she was laying out ads for the newspaper, I was sitting there making my own pretend ads." Her path to becoming a designer, however, was far from straight. Eagan went to college for math, but dropped out and moved to Mexico. "I joined a Mexican circus and performed as a trapeze artist for four months or so." After considering circus school, she decided to go to Cornish College of the Arts in Seattle and graduated with a degree in illustration.

A few years after graduating and working for various design agencies, Eagan got into the beer industry. "My husband found a Craigslist posting that said something along the lines of 'Do You Like Beer? Do You Like To Draw?'" The job was for a tap handle company appropriately named Taphandles. They were trying to morph into a design-focused company, rather than a purely manufacturing one. "I started working full-time as their sole designer. I was doing

everything from making labels to going into the garage and creating a wooden handle with a lathe and a bandsaw."

"[Taphandles] really transformed the market: A tap handle began as a functional item that someone needed to pour beer, but it became the number one marketing piece needed to sell the beer at the bar. People would request a beer based on its tap handle. Alaskan's sculpted orca tap handle prompted requests for the 'whale beer.' Tap handles began to function like billboards for what they were pouring. Tap handles became advertising, but unlike most advertising, it was the kind that people actively sought out rather than avoided. Awesome tap handles were simply selling

more beer. It's a compelling example of the selling power of design."

The craft beer industry was just beginning to grow into what it is today, and Eagan had a front row seat to the revolution. "Craft beer was booming. Many, many breweries were entering the market. It was organic that as the market was growing—and as competition grew—breweries needed more marketing support. All of a sudden, having your 'friend's-brother's-cousin who took an art class once in college' making your logo wasn't enough. Eventually, we developed an entire branding division within the company. If a brewery came to us without a strong existing brand, we could build one for them from the ground up."

As the market grew, so did Taphandles and with it its branding division. "At a certain point, we grew beyond designing for the needs of a manufacturing company. It made sense for our branding group to spin off and be our own thing." Eagan left Taphandles and started BLINDTIGER Design, a studio that specializes in the beer industry.

"We know how to design specifically for the industry—what is effective, what the market will respond to—without the pretentiousness or fluff that brewers would encounter at a nonspecialist agency. There is a genuine need for a company that specializes in what we do. There are so many nuances within all of these different breweries, within beer culture, and within beer itself. Someone from outside the craft beer industry cannot understand these intricacies the way we can. We're in the trenches with these brewers. We're part of this culture and this community. It's this closeness and understanding that enables us to communicate beer in a way that no one else can."

"The craft beer industry has grown up, and it needs someone who can support it in a professional way. Not every brewery should work with a giant agency. Those agencies work with detergent; they work with orange juice. That's not the right solution for brewers. There really is such a unique culture within beer. I mean, there's no such thing as 'orange juice

culture' or 'laundry detergent culture!' But there is beer culture, and there's an entire community built up around it."

"I can think of no other industry where there are literally hundreds of companies that are all technically doing the same thing, but they are not at all doing the same thing. Every single one of these breweries has a completely unique story, and they're expressed in such vastly different ways. There's a freedom and a playfulness in beer that you don't see in any other industry."

Design and branding play a very important role in the marketing of a product. Craft beer is not any different. "I think that consumers' expectations have grown drastically in the last year alone, and they'll only continue to grow. We had a call the other day with a brewer who said, 'When I go to a beer festival and I see my logo up against all the other breweries in my state, I feel like I'm not on the same level with them. I can't hang with them, but I want to.' This is what we're hearing—this isn't just our opinion. This is what people are calling and telling us."

Eagan has been involved in beer branding for long enough that she has seen trends come and go. She has been part of the transformation. "The communication hierarchy has been changing. What I mean by that is there have been different focuses on master brands, like Redhook for example, versus subbrands, like Longhammer IPA. Way back when, you didn't need to have a subbrand; you just had your main brand and then whatever style of beer you were selling. But then people started focusing on building entire brand personalities around one style of beer, so we started to get those really distinct, really elaborate subbrands. I think the pendulum is starting to swing back the other way now, toward investing energy in the master brand rather than in the subbrands. Especially since there are so many breweries now, having a different personality for every single beer can be too much for consumers to digest."

"Another thing that I think has been a big influence on packaging design is retail space—bottle shops, grocery stores and the like. They used to divide up their craft beer sections by type of packaging: Placing the twenty-two-ounce bottles with the twenty-two-ounce bottles, keeping the six-packs together. Now, though, a lot of them are organizing their space by beer

style. All of a sudden, one brewery's beer isn't all in the same place; it's scattered. You can no longer have the billboarding effect of your bottles all lined up. Consumers are becoming more style-focused than brewery-focused. Shelves are being rearranged to reflect that, and the breweries' packaging strategies are following."

As the industry grows, and the number of small breweries continues to increase, Eagan believes we are looking at a pre-Prohibition landscape. "There are just going to be so many more breweries. I think the idea of 'Success = Bigger' will start to go away, though, because everyone can't do that successfully. I'd like to see people actually own the idea of being local—to truly own it." ●

Bale Breaker Brewing Co.
Moxee, Washington
BaleBreaker.com

Design by BLINDTIGER Design
Seattle, Washington
BlindtigerDesign.com

Yakima Craft Brewing Co.
Yakima, Washington
yakimacraftbrewing.com
Design by Yakima Craft Brewing Co.

CraftHaus Brewery
Las Vegas, Nevada
crafthausbrewery.com

Design by Daniel Bellon
Pittsburgh, Pennsylvania
dbellon.com

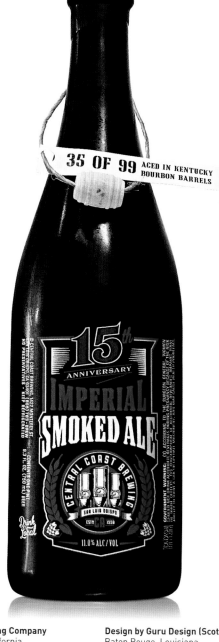

Redhook Brewery
Woodinville, Washington
Redhook.com

Design by Sam Robinette
Portland, Oregon
AccidentalColor.com

Central Coast Brewing Company
San Luis Obispo, California
CentralCoastBrewing.com

Design by Guru Design (Scott Greci)
Baton Rouge, Louisiana
GuruDesignCo.com

Almanac Beer Co.
San Francisco, California
AlmanacBeer.com
Design by Almanac Beer Co. (Damian Fagan)

Elysian Brewing Company
Seattle, Washington
ElysianBrewing.com
Design by Elysian Brewing (Corinne McNielly)

FiftyFifty Brewing Co.
Truckee, California
FiftyFiftyBrewing.com

Design by Blase Design (Aimee Blase)
Truckee, California / Austin, Texas
BlaseDesign.com

HOPPY THE WOODSMAN

A rich oak-aged beer with a light hop note and strong toasty malt character. Aroma results from the seamless blend of vanilla, caramel, brandied cherry and Yakima Valley hops. Flavors of caramel and oak are offset by the warmth of alcohol. A perfect winter warmer that is well balanced to the end.

Schooner Exact Brewing Co.
Seattle, Washington
schoonerexact.com

Design by BLINDTIGER Design
Seattle, Washington
BlindtigerDesign.com

10 Barrel Brewing Company
Bend, Oregon
10barrel.com

Created and Designed by Wildland Creative Co.
Portland, Oregon
WildlandCo.com

THE WEST

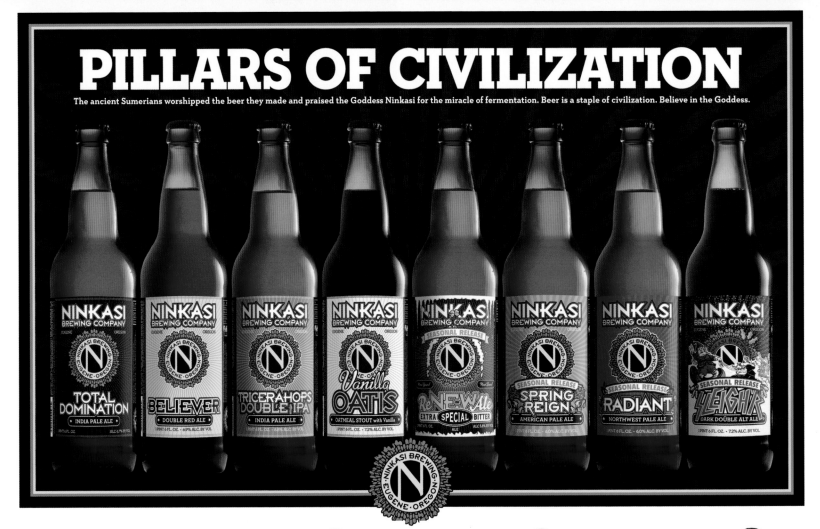

Ninkasi Brewing Company
Eugene, Oregon
NinkasiBrewing.com
Design by Ninkasi (Tony Figoli)

Bitter Old Fecker Rustic Ales
Chelsea, Michigan

Design by Neltner Small Batch
Camp Springs, Kentucky
NeltnerSmallBatch.com

02 The Middle

IPA2 is our imperial IPA, a beer of flux and spring. Its bitter first taste a memory of winter's chill, the bravado of Nugget, Summit, and CTZ hops, it ends welcomingly sweet and smooth, the effort of a decoction mash. Our Amber, Gold, and Pale malts roasted in house create a raw character, marked by a thawing of hope, anticipation for open spaces, wild air, and the arrival of protracted evenings in porches. Dry hopped with equal parts CTZ and Willamette for a floral finish.

OMF MALT & BREW

IPA2

8% ABV / 105 IBU | LIMITED BATCH

BOTTLE NUMBER

SEALED DATE

BREWED & BOTTLED BY • OMF M&B
2810 LARIMER ST • DENVER, CO 80205

OMFMB.COM

1 PINT, 6 FL OZ / 650ML

Our Mutual Friend Malt & Brew
Denver, Colorado
omfmb.com

Design by Justin Pervorse
Atlanta, Georgia
JustinPervorse.com

COOL BEER LABELS

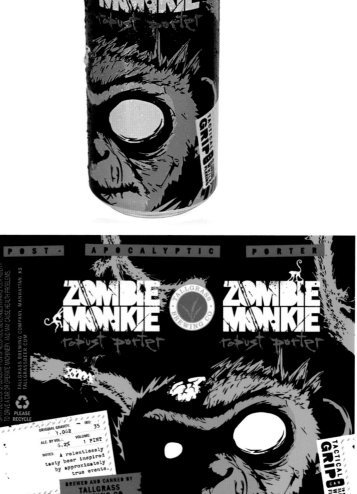

Tallgrass Brewing Company
Manhattan, Kansas
TallgrassBeer.com
Design by Tallgrass Brewing Company

COOL BEER LABELS

Hinterland Brewery
Green Bay, Wisconsin
HinterlandBeer.com

Design by Woodchuck Creative (Chuck Lacasse)
Onalaska, Wisconsin
WoodchuckCreative.com

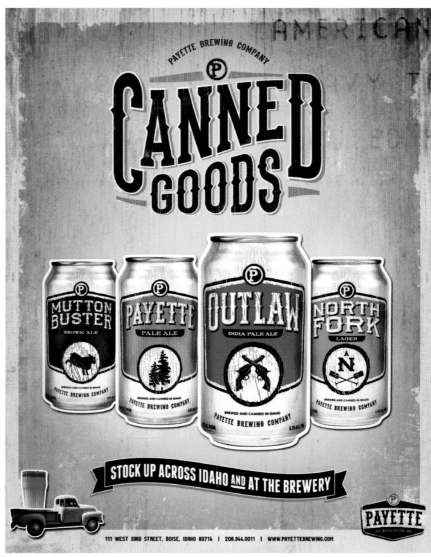

Payette Brewing Company
Garden City, Idaho
PayetteBrewing.com

Design by Drake Cooper
Boise, Idaho
DrakeCooper.com

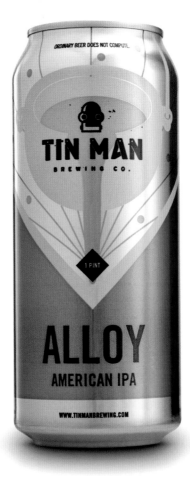

Tin Man Brewing Co.
Evansville, Indiana
TinManBrewing.com

Design by Aaron Tanner & Matt Wagner
MelodicVirtue.com / wgnrdsgn.com

Great Divide Brewing Company
Denver, Colorado
GreatDivide.com

Design by Cultivator Advertising and Design
Denver, Colorado
CultivatorAds.com

New Belgium Brewing
Fort Collins, Colorado
NewBelgium.com
Design by New Belgium Brewing (Melyssa Mead, Jodi Taylor)

Two Brothers Brewing Company
Warrenville, Illinois
TwoBrothersBrewing.com
Design by Two Brothers Brewing Company

Upslope Brewing Company
Boulder, Colorado
UpslopeBrewing.com

Design by Anthem Branding
Boulder, Colorado
AnthemBranding.com

Left Hand Brewing Co.
Longmont, Colorado
LeftHandBrewing.com

Design By Moxie Sozo (Charles Bloom & Nate Dyer)
Boulder, Colorado
MoxieSozo.com

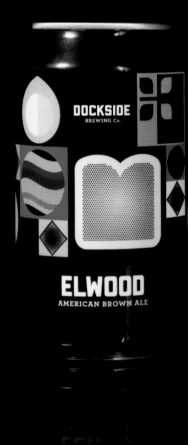

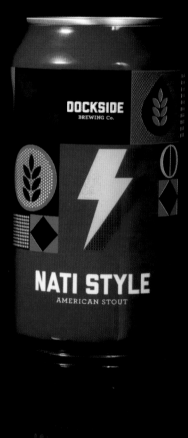

Dockside Brewing Co.
Cincinnati, Ohio
Facebook.com/docksidebrewing

Design by Landor Associates (Greg Althoff)
Cincinnati, Ohio
Landor.com

Rush River Brewing Company
River Falls, Wisconsin
RushRiverBeer.com

Design by Westwerk
Minneapolis, Minnesota
Westwerk.com

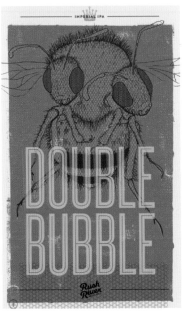

Furthermore Beer
Spring Green, Wisconsin
FurthermoreBeer.com

Design by Erin Fuller
Madison, Wisconsin
ErinFullerGraphics.com

51

THE MIDDLE

Three Floyds Brewing
Munster, Indiana
3Floyds.com

Design by Zimmer-Design
Chicago, Illinois
Zimmer-Design.com

MadTree Brewing Company
Cincinnati, Ohio
MadTreeBrewing.com

Design by Project Red (John Pattison)
Cincinnati, Ohio
JohnPattison.Viewbook.com/John_Pattison

North Peak Brewing Company
Traverse City, Michigan
NorthPeakBeer.com

Design by Northern United Brewing Co.
Ann Arbor, Michigan

Half Acre Beer Company
Chicago, Illinois

Design by Phineas X. Jones
Chicago, Illinois

Odell Brewing Co.
Fort Collins, Colorado
OdellBrewing.com

Design by TBD Agency
Bend, Oregon
TBDagency.com

57

THE MIDDLE

COOL BEER LABELS

Aspen Brewing Company
Aspen, Colorado
AspenBrewingCompany.com

Design by Jeremy Elder
Minneapolis, Minnesota
JeremyElder.com

O'Fallon Brewery for Bailey's Chocolate Bar
St. Louis, Missouri
BaileysChocolateBar.com

Design by TOKY Branding + Design
St. Louis, Missouri
toky.com

CLOWN SHOES

CLOWN SHOES

Intense flavors, reminiscent of candied fruits, mix with American hops and sweet orange peel to create a unique take on a Belgian-Style Ale.

Disclaimer: No muffin tops were harmed in the production of this label.

1 pint, 6 fl. oz.
Alc. 10% by volume

Ale brewed with natural flavor

Mercury Brewing Co., Ipswich, MA

FL CT-MA-ME-NY
OR-VT-5¢ DEP
MI 10¢ OK CA CRV

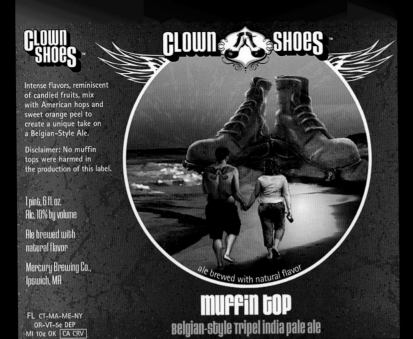

ale brewed with natural flavor

muffin top
Belgian-style Tripel india pale ale

CLOWN SHOES

CLOWN SHOES

Hoppy Feet guy extinguished evil via a sharp stake through an undead chest. Now, Blaecorn Unidragon, full of fury, has expelled another bloodsucker from Earth. We hate vampires, but love Vampire Slayer, which we blended in equal parts with Blaecorn Unidragon, bourbon barrel aging the mix to beget Very Angry Beast.

1 pint, 6 fl. oz.
Alc. 11.5% by volume

Stout aged in bourbon barrels

Mercury Brewing Co., Ipswich, MA

FL CT-MA-ME-NY
OR-VT-5¢ DEP
MI 10¢ OK CA CRV

very Angry Beast
American imperial stout
Stout aged in bourbon barrels

Clown Shoes Beer
Ipswich, Massachusetts
ClownShoesBeer.com

Design by Stacey George
Massachusetts
StaceyGeorge.com

03 The East

Carton Brewing
Atlantic Highlands, New Jersey
CartonBrewing.com

Design by Rendition Designs
New Jersey
RenditionDesigns.com

Photography by Brian Casse

Relic Brewing Company
Plainville, Connecticut

Mark Sigman, founder and head brewer of Relic Brewing, has always been an avid traveler. In the fall of 1993, while traveling out west, he became increasingly interested in craft beer and brewing. Once he settled in Jackson Hole, Wyoming, he ordered his first craft beer kit and started brewing at home. After a few years, Sigman took the leap and Relic Brewing Company was born.

Relic is unique in that they don't just make hop-based beers. Their beer is mostly what Sigman calls Belgian/American hybrids. Having traveled to Belgium twice, once solely for beer tasting, Sigman found that these were the styles he was drawn to. "I have always enjoyed Belgian and farmhouse-style ales. I found that these types were both well received, quite interestingly, and the ones I was taking home the most."

Flavor was not the only inspiration Sigman received while traveling. He also credits his international travels with the naming of the brewery. "I really enjoy exploring ancient archaeological sites across the globe. At most of them, there are relics related to beer or beer like substances, such as stone contracts, earthenware vessels and much more."

The names of the beers are as interesting and complex as the taste of the brews themselves, and they're a balance between keeping with the Relic theme and selecting what tastes and feels right for each beer. "Sometimes I come up with the recipe and style and just start brainstorming names that make sense, like with Thrice, a Belgian triple; I like Old English and the

medieval period, so I thought *thrice*, like Old English for three, and in turn came up with the Illumination concept which, was how the monks wrote in the medieval period. I had seen many of these rare books across Europe and was always fascinated; this leads to the Relic story eventually. Sometimes, I just brainstorm names, and cool ideas, and then that will become a beer. Like The Witching Hour or Darkness Falls or The Falconess, or Queen Anne's Revenge."

The diversity in the design of labels and the names of beers makes Relic stand out. Sigman is proud to employ many different designers to create labels for his brewery. "I like the range of looks and enjoy giving people a chance, even if some are better than others." For the names of his beers, Sigman finds naming each brew an enjoyable outlet for his creativity. "I enjoy the creativity of naming the beers and coming up with appropriate themes and cool concepts. Most of the time, I come up with the concept, but occasionally, I will be over-ruled by the artist." ✎

Relic Brewing
Plainville, Connecticut
RelicBeer.com

Madeline design by Samela Aguirre
Farmingdale NY
www.samelaart.com

Thrice design by Kristen Mixter
Avon, CT

Fortnight design by Ito Pizarro
East Hartford, Connecticut
ItoPizarro.com

Nano-A-Nano design by Gary Holmes
West Hartford, Connecticut
Gariphic.com

Photography by Kathryn Speeg
SweetPeaPic.com

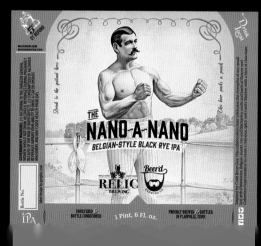

Baxter Brewing Co.
Lewiston, Maine
BaxterBrewing.com
Design by Baxter Brewing (Joshua Fisher)

Blue Mountain Barrel House
Arlington, Virginia
BlueMountainBarrel.com

Design by Watermark Design
Charlottesville, Virginia
DesignByWatermark.com

Monocacy Brewing Company
Frederick, Maryland
MonocacyBrewing.com

Design by Tribe
Frederick, Maryland
Tribecol.com

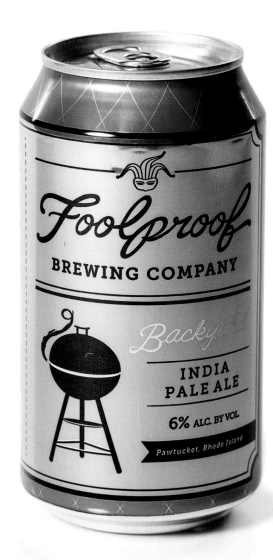

Foolproof Brewing Company
Pawtucket, Rhode Island
FoolproofBrewing.com

Design by Elizabeth Weinberg
New York, New York
ElizabethAtlas.com

Full Pint Brewing Company
North Versailles, Pennsylvania
FullPintBrewing.com

Design by Phil Seth (Forbidden Ink)
Avalon, Pennsylvania
PhilSethDesign.com - ForbiddenInk.com

The Alchemist
Waterbury, Vermont
AlchemistBeer.com

Design by Dan Blakeslee
Somerville, Massachusetts
DanBlakeslee.com

The Bronx Brewery
Bronx, New York
TheBronxBrewery.com
Design by The Bronx Brewery

Photography by Alan Gastelum
Brooklyn, New York
AlanGastelum.com

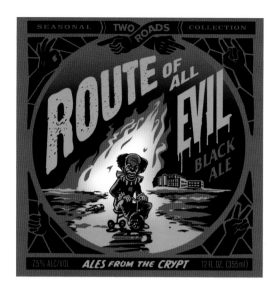

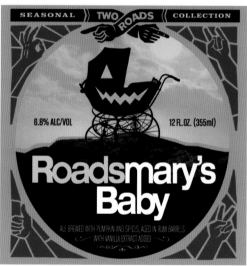

Two Roads Brewing Company
Stratford, Connecticut
TwoRoadsBrewing.com

Design by BRZoom, LLC
Baton Rouge, Louisianna / Wilton, Connecticut
BRZoom.com

Sixpoint Brewery

Brooklyn, New York

Sixpoint is one of the best-distributed and most recognizable craft breweries on the East Coast. Their signature four-packs of cans have become a favorite among beer fans. Their packaging is bold, clean and includes all the brewing stats along the bottom, in a nicely designed grid. Aaron Ekroth, Sixpoint's creative director, explains, "We always wanted to offer key indicators beyond just volume and alcohol by volume (ABV). By offering the International Bitterness Units (IBU) indicator, beer lovers can get a sense of the flavor; and given that our packaging is opaque and protects beer from light, the Standard Reference Method (SRM) indicates the color of the beer." Another strong piece in their design is the icon or medallion for each beer. Ekroth says each of them is intended to transmit the essence of the beer into a single image.

Brewing wise, Sixpoint take pride in not adhering to the traditional style guidelines.

"When we began brewing, we were less interested in brewing 'to style' for easy categorization in age-old categories. Rather, with creations like Sweet Action, we have allowed ourselves a full creative license to brew what inspires us without great concern for style categories. If you are curious about what style a beer may be, we can offer you this, with a smile: 'It's a Sixpoint.'"

Sixpoint Brewery
Brooklyn, New York
Sixpoint.com

Design by Nate Garn
Stoughton, Wisconsin
NateGarn.com

Photography by Michael Harlan Turkell
HarlanTurk.com

Union Craft Brewing
Baltimore, Maryland
UnionCraftBrewing.com

Design by Gilah Press + Design
Baltimore, Maryland
GilahPress.com

New England Brewing Company
Woodbridge, Connecticut
NewEnglandBrewing.com

Design by Craig Gilbert
West Haven, Connecticut
ThatCraigGuy.com

St. Boniface Craft Brewing Company
Ephrata, Pennsylvania
facebook.com/StBonifaceBrewing

Design by ADG Creative
Columbia, Maryland
ADGcreative.net

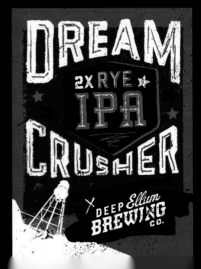

04 The South

Red Brick Brewing
Atlanta, Georgia
RedBrickBrewing.com

Design by 22squared
Atlanta, Georgia / Tampa, Florida
22squared.com

Tin Roof Brewing Co.
Baton Rouge, Louisiana
TinRoofBeer.com

Design by Unreal [Rick Dobbs]
New Orleans, Louisiana
UnrealLLC.com

Craft and Growler Beer Filling Station
Dallas, Texas
CraftAndGrowler.com

Design by Caliber Creative
Dallas, Texas
CaliberCreative.com

Saint Arnold Brewing Company
Houston, Texas
SaintArnold.com

Design by Primer Grey
Houston, Texas
PrimerGrey.com

The Steel Brewing Company
Longview, Texas

Design by Turner Duckworth
San Francisco, California
TurnerDuckworth.com

Big Boss Brewing Co.
Raleigh, North Carolina
BigBossBrewing.com

Design by McKinney (Scott Pridgen)
Durham, North Carolina
McKinney.com / ScottPridgen.com

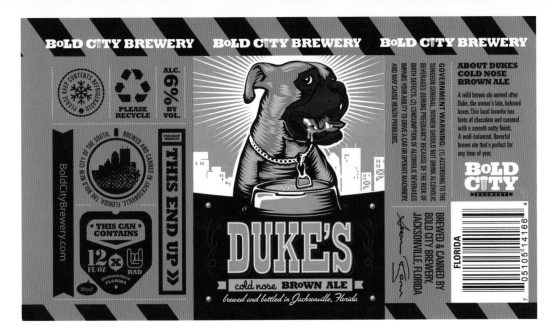

Bold City Brewing
Jacksonville, Florida

Bold City Brewing is a family-run brewery founded by former homebrewer Brian Miller and his mother Susan.

The Millers are proud to be part of the craft beer community in Jacksonville, so when they enlisted designer Kendrick Kidd to create their labels, they already had a few ideas in mind. "Their biggest priority was paying homage to their ties with Jacksonville, Florida," Kidd says. "The skyline has a cameo appearance on every can design. Bold City requested this from the very first meeting. It's been a challenge at times to find a spot for downtown Jacksonville that makes sense on every design, but it's a challenge we're happy to take on."

Kidd's design has a retro color palette to instill a sense of history, but he also introduced bright colors to accentuate the name of the brewery. "The result is a color range as diverse and unique as the beer offerings, but they still present as a unified family."

The label for Duke's Cold Nose Brown Ale features the brewmaster's dog, a friendly boxer named Duke, who was the official greeter at the brewery. In order to immortalize the canine on the can, Kidd staged a photo session with Duke and based the detailed illustration on one of the photographs. Kidd admits he wasn't sure this more realistic style of illustration would fit with the other two can designs. "We were a little nervous at first, but in the end it's added to the charm and authenticity of the series." A dog, a manatee and a whale: a match made in beer heaven. ✒

Bold City Brewery
Jacksonville, Florida
BoldCityBrewery.com

Design by Shepherd
Jacksonville, Florida
Shepherd-Agency.com

Weaver Brew Co.
Houston, Texas
WeaverBrew.co

Design by Sputnik Creative
Austin, Texas
SputnikCreative.com

COOL BEER LABELS

Back Forty Beer Company
Gadsden, Alabama
BackFortyBeer.com

Design by MindVolt
Athens, Alabama
MindVolt.com

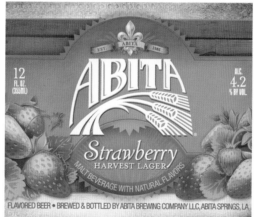

Abita Brewing Company
Abita Springs, Louisiana
Abita.com

Monday Night Brewing
Atlanta, Georgia
MondayNightBrewing.com
Design by Monday Night Brewing

Chase the Rabbit!

Red Hare
BREWING COMPANY
Marietta, GA

Long Day Lager

Bohemian Style Lager

Gangway IPA

Watership Brown Ale

Red Hare

Stowaway IPA

India Pale Ale

Red Hare

Whabbit Wheat

American Wheat Ale

Lonerider
Brewing Company
Raleigh, North Carolina

Lonerider Brewing Company is one of the many craft breweries in the country that is making the shift from their original branding and packaging to a more sophisticated look in an effort to stand out from other craft beers. This redesign, however, kept the overall brand and its original concept. Sumit Vohra, chief executive officer of Lonerider, wanted the concept of Western outlaws to remain as the basis of Lonerider. He just needed someone to come in and polish the original design and take it to the next level. Vohra hired Clean Design, a Raleigh marketing and branding design firm, and in turn, Jon Parker to help with this process.

Parker watched a great deal of old Western movies and examined old Western movie posters for research and inspiration. Since Lonerider wanted a more modern appeal, Clean Design brought in illustrator Jeff Winstead and asked him to update each character on the labels using bold colors, creating contrast between lights and darks, and using outlines similar to those of a graphic novel. "Once we started getting the art from Jeff, we felt we really had something great—a modern take on Old West outlaws that felt fresh and that everyone could relate to." Says Parker. "The characters that are assigned to each beer do portray certain Western stereotypes—the peacemaking sheriff, the Annie Oakley, the gun-toting tough gal, and the seductive salon girl with a heart of gold." Who would expect anything different from a brewery called Lonerider? ●

Lonerider Brewing Company
Raleigh, North Carolina
LoneRiderBeer.com

Design by Clean Design
Raleigh, North Carolina
CleanDesign.com

Illustration by Jeff Winstead
Greensboro, North Carolina
JeffWinstead.com

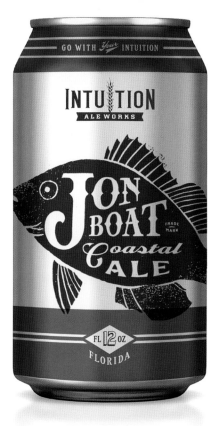

Intuition Ale Works
Jacksonville, Florida
IntuitionAleWorks.com

Design by DeRouen & Co
Austin, Texas
DeRouenCo.com

Foothills Brewing
Winston-Salem, North Carolina
FoothillsBrewing.com

Design by ShapiroWalker Design
Winston-Salem, North Carolina
ShapiroWalker.com

Mystery Brewing Co.
Hillsborough, North Carolina
MysteryBrewing.com

Design by BLINDTIGER Design
Seattle, Washington
BlindtigerDesign.com

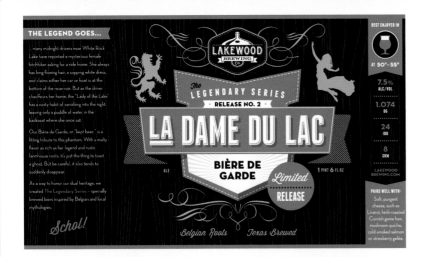

... many midnight drivers near White Rock Lake have reported a mysterious female hitchhiker asking for a ride home. She always has long flowing hair, a sopping white dress, and claims either her car or boat is at the bottom of the reservoir. But as the driver chauffeurs her home, the "Lady of the Lake" has a nasty habit of vanishing into the night, leaving only a puddle of water in the backseat where she once sat.

Our Bière de Garde, or "kept beer," is a fitting tribute to this phantom. With a malty flavor as rich as her legend and rustic, farmhouse roots, it's just the thing to toast a ghost. But be careful, it also tends to suddenly disappear.

As a way to honor our dual heritage, we created The Legendary Series — specially brewed biers inspired by Belgian and local mythologies.

Schol!

The LEGENDARY SERIES
RELEASE NO. 2

LA DAME DU LAC

BIÈRE DE GARDE

Limited RELEASE

LAKEWOOD BREWING Co.

BEST ENJOYED IN

AT 50°–55°

7.5% ALC/VOL

1.074 OG

24 IBU

8 SRM

ALE

1 PINT 6 FL OZ

LAKEWOOD BREWING.COM

PAIRS WELL WITH: Soft, pungent cheese, such as Livarot, herb-roasted Cornish game hen, mushroom quiche, cold-smoked salmon or strawberry gelée.

Belgian Roots • Texas Brewed

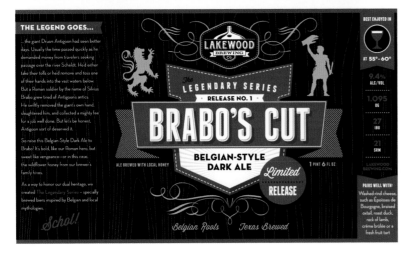

... the giant Druon Antigoon had seen better days. Usually the time passed quickly as he demanded money from travelers seeking passage over the river Scheldt. He'd either take their tolls or he'd remove and toss one of their hands into the vast waters below. But a Roman soldier by the name of Silvius Brabo grew tired of Antigoon's antics. He swiftly removed the giant's own hand, slaughtered him, and collected a mighty fee for a job well done. But let's be honest, Antigoon sort of deserved it.

So raise this Belgian-Style Dark Ale to Brabo! It's bold, like our Roman hero, but sweet like vengeance—or in this case, the wildflower honey from our brewer's family hives.

As a way to honor our dual heritage, we created The Legendary Series — specially brewed biers inspired by Belgian and local mythologies.

Schol!

The LEGENDARY SERIES
RELEASE NO. 1

BRABO'S CUT

BELGIAN-STYLE DARK ALE

Limited RELEASE

LAKEWOOD BREWING Co.

BEST ENJOYED IN

AT 55°–60°

9.4% ALC/VOL

1.095 OG

27 IBU

21 SRM

ALE BREWED WITH LOCAL HONEY

1 PINT 6 FL OZ

LAKEWOOD BREWING.COM

PAIRS WELL WITH: Washed-rind cheese, such as Époisses de Bourgogne, braised oxtail, roast duck, rack of lamb, crème brûlée or a fresh fruit tart

Belgian Roots • Texas Brewed

96

Lakewood Brewing Company
Garland, Texas
LakewoodBrewing.com

Design by Tracy Locke
(Tyler Kitchens & Craig Bradley)
Dallas, Texas
TracyLocke.com

NoDa Brewing Company
Charlotte, North Carolina
NoDaBrewing.com

Design by Saturday Brand Communications
Charlotte, North Carolina
HeySaturday.com

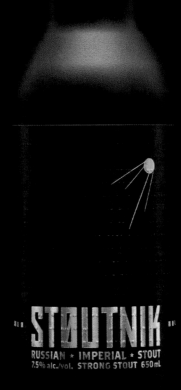

Longwood Brewery
Nanaimo, British Columbia, Canada
LongwoodBeer.com

Design by Hired Guns Creative
Nanaimo, British Columbia, Canada
HiredGunsCreative.com

05 The Americas

Cervecería Pública Condesa
México D.F., México
cpubc.mx

Design by Cuatro Estudio
(Luis Ariza/Mauricio Fernández)
Ensenada, Baja California, México

Muskoka Brewery
Bracebridge, Ontario, Canada
MuskokaBrewery.com

Design by Rethink Canada (Jeff Harrison)
Vancouver / Toronto, Canada
RethinkCanada.com

Muskoka Brewery
Bracebridge, Ontario, Canada
MuskokaBrewery.com

Design by Rethink Canada (Jeff Harrison)
Vancouver / Toronto, Canada
RethinkCanada.com

À l'abri de la Tempête
Magdalen Islands, Québec, Canada
AlabridelaTempete.com

Design by Nuev Design (Martin Fiset)
Magdalen Islands, Québec, Canada
NuevDesign.com

Fábricas Nacionales de Cerveza S.A.
Montevideo, Uruguay
Pilsen.com.uy

Design by Havas WW Gurisa (Rodrigo Granese)
Montevideo, Uruguay
CargoCollective.com/RodrigoGranese

THE AMERICAS

IndHED
Porto Alegre, Brazil

Eduardo Andrade and João Francisco Hack are partners in IndustriaHED, a design studio in the south of Brazil. So how do two guys go from running a design business to making beer? Well, it all started with happy hour every Friday. All the employees would get together and celebrate a week's work with beer and some food. Andrade and Hack then decided that the studio should make its own beer. Andrade says, "The primary idea was to have a beer for family, friends and clients." The beer took off and now they are producing 1,200 liters (317 gallons) per month. That's two thousand 600-milliliter bottles, more than enough for family, friends and clients.

As a designer, Andrade sees the role of design in the success of IndHED very clearly. "In the first month we launched the product for family and friends, but ended up getting over 2,000 orders from the whole country. People hadn't even tried the beer, but they already wanted to buy it. The design is really what's making IndHED well known. The reason you buy a product that you don't know is because the way the packaging looks. If you really want to have a kick-ass product, you need great package design."

The guys know design, but left the beer stuff to a professional. "Marcus Gazolla, master brewer at Imaculada Brewery in Caxias do Sul, about eighty miles north of Porto Alegre, came up with the recipe considering flavor, aroma, bitterness, drinkability and color." IndHED is an American pale ale made using three types of Belgian malt and two types of American hops.

Like everywhere else, the craft beer industry is growing in southern Brazil. More and more brands are popping up everywhere and the competition is getting tight. IndHED, however, isn't concerned. "The market is getting very competitive," says Andrade, "but we stand out with quality of our beer and, of course, our strong branding." ●

Bogotá Beer Company
Bogotá, Colombia
BogotaBeerCompany.com

Design by Lip Ltda.
Bogotá, Colombia
LuchoCorrea.com

Double Vienna
Morada Cia Etílica
Curitiba, Paraná, Brasil
MoradaCervejaria.com.br

Design by D-lab
Curitiba, Paraná, Brasil
dlab.com.br

Brisset Beer Company
Montreal, Quebec, Canada
BiereBrisset.com

Design by Carte Blanche and Scenario A
Montreal, Quebec, Canada
cbcm.ca / ScenarioA.ca

Cervejaria Heidelberg
F#%*ing Beer
Curitiba, Paraná, Brasil
FuckingBeer.com

Design by D-lab
Curitiba, Paraná, Brasil
dlab.com.br

THE AMERICAS

La Consigne Beer Chope
Montreal, Canada

Looking more like an upscale bike shop than a beer store, La Consigne is a specialty craft beer and microbrewery store in the Ahuntsic district in the northern part of Montreal. The shop opened its doors in December 2011 and has an impressive selection of Québécois craft beers.

Designer and part-owner Yanick Nolet is responsible for the branding of the store. He says the design "is really important, because that is what makes us different and unique." The bike shop look is no coincidence: Nolet is an avid cyclist. "We wanted the design to have the cycling spirit." The logo is a bottle opener on one side and a cycling fifteen-millimeter wrench on the other. Nolet says that the shop has become a usual stop for cyclists during long rides who come in and grab a beer on their way home. ●

LIFE IS TOO SHORT TO DRINK CHEAP BEER

La Consigne
Montreal, Québec, Canada
LaConsigne.ca

Design by Noly (Yanick Nolet)
Montreal, Québec, Canada
Noly.ca

Lumber Jack

Quand Gros Mollet rencontre son chum Jack, venu directement du Tennessee, c'est pour la grande virée. Rondeur du malt caramel, fût vanillé et parfums de bourbon sont au rendez-vous!

GROS MOLLET

bière extra-forte vieillie en fût de bourbon • extra strong ale aged in oak bourbon barrels

MICROBRASSERIE DU LAC SAINT-JEAN

9,0% alc./vol. 500 mL

8,0% alc./vol. 500 mL

TanTe TricoTanTe

bière triple • triple ale

MICROBRASSERIE DU LAC ST-JEAN

5,5% alc./vol. 500 mL

ViRe-CaPoT

bière blonde • blond ale

MICROBRASSERIE DU LAC ST-JEAN

7,8% alc./vol. 500 mL

GRoS MoLLeT

bière brune forte • strong brown ale

MICROBRASSERIE DU LAC ST-JEAN

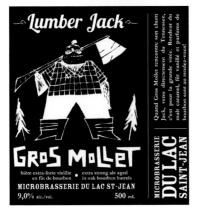

6,5% alc./vol. 500 mL

Cache-à-épices

bière forte • strong ale

MICROBRASSERIE DU LAC ST-JEAN

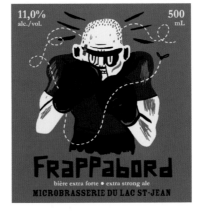

11,0% alc./vol. 500 mL

FraPPaboRd

bière extra forte • extra strong ale

MICROBRASSERIE DU LAC ST-JEAN

5,1% alc./vol. 500 mL

bouTeFeU

bière rousse • red ale

MICROBRASSERIE DU LAC ST-JEAN

Microbrasserie du Lac Saint-Jean
St-Gédéon, Québec, Canada
MicroduLac.com

Design & Illustration by Patrick Doyon
Montréal, Québec, Canada
Doiion.com

Russell Brewing Company
Surrey, British Columbia, Canada
RussellBeer.com

Design by Atmosphere Design
Vancouver, British Columbia, Canada
AtmosphereDesign.ca

Sheken
El Hoyo, Argentina
Sheken.com.ar

Design by Tridimage
Buenos Aires, Argentina
tridimage.com

Russell Brewing Company
Surrey, British Columbia, Canada
RussellBeer.com

Design by Atmosphere Design
Vancouver, British Columbia, Canada
AtmosphereDesign.ca

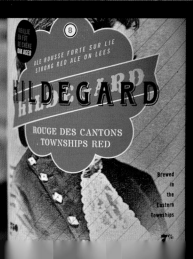

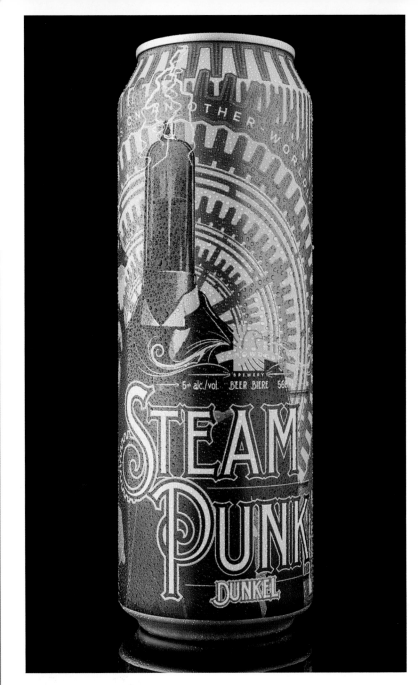

Longwood Brewery
Nanaimo, British Columbia, Canada
LongwoodBeer.com

Design by Hired Guns Creative
Nanaimo, British Columbia, Canada
HiredGunsCreative.com

Backus
Cuzco, Perú
CusquenaBeer.com

Design by Tridimage
Buenos Aires, Argentina
tridimage.com

Las Bruscas
Caviahue, Argentina
facebook.com/lasbruscascerveza.caviahue

Design by Tridimage
Buenos Aires, Argentina
tridimage.com

THE AMERICAS

Underground Beer Club
Montevideo, Uruguay
UBC.com.uy

Design by Mundial (Martín Azambuja & Francisco Cunha)
Montevideo, Uruguay
Mundial.uy

BRASSÉES
AVEC DES
MALTS DU
QUÉBEC

PORTER BALTIQUE
LAGER NOIRE · BLACK LAGER

BIÈRE EXTRA-FORTE
EXTRA-STRONG BEER
750 mL

WEIZENBOCK
BRUNE DE BLÉ · DARK WHEAT ALE

BIÈRE EXTRA-FORTE
EXTRA-STRONG BEER
750 mL

DOPPELBOCK
LAGER BRUNE · DARK LAGER

BIÈRE EXTRA-FORTE
EXTRA-STRONG BEER
750 mL

Les Trois Mousquetaires Microbrasseurs
Brossard, Québec, Canada
LesTroisMousquetaires.ca
Design by Les Trois Mousquetaires Microbrasseurs

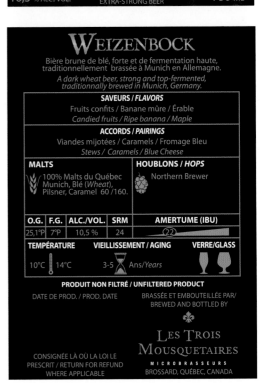

GRANDE CUVÉE

WEIZENBOCK
BRUNE DE BLÉ · DARK WHEAT ALE

10,5 % ALC./VOL.   BIÈRE EXTRA-FORTE
EXTRA-STRONG BEER   750 mL

WEIZENBOCK

Bière brune de blé, forte et de fermentation haute,
traditionnellement brassée à Munich en Allemagne.
*A dark wheat beer, strong and top-fermented,
traditionnally brewed in Munich, Germany.*

SAVEURS / FLAVORS
Fruits confits / Banane mûre / Érable
Candied fruits / Ripe banana / Maple

ACCORDS / PAIRINGS
Viandes mijotées / Caramels / Fromage Bleu
Stews / Caramels / Blue Cheese

MALTS	HOUBLONS / HOPS
100% Malts du Québec Munich, Blé (*Wheat*), Pilsner, Caramel 60 /160.	Northern Brewer

O.G.	F.G.	ALC./VOL.	SRM	AMERTUME (IBU)
25,1°P	7°P	10,5 %	24	22

TEMPÉRATURE	VIEILLISSEMENT / AGING	VERRE/GLASS
10°C 14°C	3-5 Ans/Years	

PRODUIT NON FILTRÉ / UNFILTERED PRODUCT

DATE DE PROD. / PROD. DATE   BRASSÉE ET EMBOUTEILLÉE PAR/
BREWED AND BOTTLED BY

**LES TROIS
MOUSQUETAIRES**
MICROBRASSEURS
BROSSARD, QUÉBEC, CANADA

CONSIGNÉE LÀ OÙ LA LOI LE
PRESCRIT / RETURN FOR REFUND
WHERE APPLICABLE

Beau's All Natural Brewing Co.
Vankleek Hill, Ontario, Canada
Beaus.ca
Design by Beau's All Natural Brewing Co.

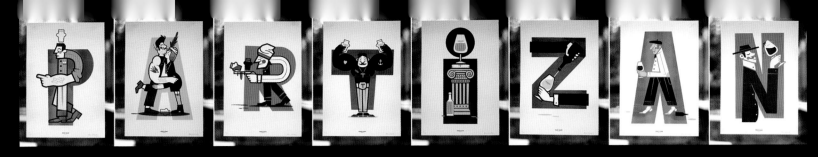

06 The United Kingdom

Brew by Numbers
London, England
BrewByNumbers.com

Design by Duke Harper
Southwark, London, England
DukeHarper.com

THE
CELT
EXPERIENCE
SEP? 2007 EST?

The Celt Experience
Caerphilly, Wales
CeltExperience.com

Design by Kutchibok Limited
Cardiff, Wales
Kutchibok.co.uk

DARK–O
ABV 4.1%
500ML

OTLEY O1
ABV 4.0%
500ML

Otley Brewing Company
OtleyBrewing.co.uk
Pontypridd, Wales

Design by Smorgasbord Studio
SmorgasbordStudio.com
Cardiff, Wales

Quaffing Gravy
Bradford, England

"Let's make some beer and do cool shit."

With those few proverbial words Quaffing Gravy was born. When asked if Quaffing Gravy is a standard microbrewery, owner Ben Gravy is clear: "I guess we're like a standard microbrewery in size." But that's where the comparisons pretty much stop. The statement on their website sums it up this way: "We believe not only in getting the inside right, but also in getting the outside right. So we've created a crisp, clean, delicately hopped, easy drinking pale ale and gone to the lengths of designing a screen printed bottle."

The design and feel of the bottle is just the beginning. Their website, their T-shirts and the overall aesthetic of the brand is definitively part of the experience. It's more than just the beer. "Design runs throughout everything we do," Gravy says. "We have a love for great design and wanted to bring that into the beer. We always try put that extra effort in, which is particularly evident in our bottles. We could have done a label but we were always going to go with a screen-printed bottle. Yes it's more expensive, yes it's a bit awkward to do; but, quite honestly, it's just cooler." To achieve the cool factor, they approached designers Mark Yates and Dr. Roy. Gravy explains, "We wanted the design to be handdrawn. That's when we collaborated with Mark and Dr. Roy— they're both good friends of ours. We talked with Mark about what we wanted and how we wanted the logo to look: the style, the feel, how it would be printed, etc. He then came back with exactly what we had in our heads. We then added the little flash, and we'd found our identity. Then Dr. Roy helped us with the handdrawn font. We didn't just want a standard font; we wanted something unique. Dr. Roy nailed it. It just works beautifully. It's hard to describe what Roy did, but the type he created looks how we speak, if you get what I mean."

And future plans for these off-beat beer guys? "We've got some pretty nice ideas of what we want to do next," Gravy says. "Of course, it will be something quaffable." Of course. ●

The Private Brewery of BoB
St Albans, England
BoB-Brewery.co.uk

Design by Distil Studio
St Albans, England
DistilStudio.co.uk

A Conversation with James Watt, Captain and Co-Founder of BrewDog

BrewDog was founded in 2007 in the town of Fraserburgh, on the Eastern coast of Scotland, by James Watt and Martin Dickie. In 2012, they moved their operation a few miles south to Ellon. BrewDog has become Scotland's largest independently owned brewery producing about 120,000 bottles per month for export all over the world. They are one of the most notorious and controversial breweries in the United Kingdom. Steven Speeg sat down with James Watt and they discussed phones falling into beer, taxidermy and the controversy that seems to follow BrewDog everywhere they go.

How did you and Martin meet?

Martin and I met at school and were mates as teenagers. When we both finished university, we became good friends, bonding over a passion for great beer and a mutual frustration at the industrially brewed lagers and stuffy ales that dominated the UK market.

Did you homebrew before you leaped into professional craft brewing?

The very first BrewDog beers were created in Martin's garage. We would brew small-scale batches of experimental beer, fill bottles by hand and sell them at local markets out of the back of our van. There was a lot of trial and error, but it was awesome to be making our own beer.

The brewery was named after an actual dog. Can you tell us a little about him?

The inspiration for the name was Bracken, my dog. When we first launched, the whole team was just Martin, Bracken and me. The name seemed to fit what we were all about.

In 2007 when you opened BrewDog, did you dream that the brewery would become so successful so quickly?

The growth of BrewDog has been insane. We knew there was a thirst for great beer, but we never expected it to take off like it has. The huge response, both in the UK and around the world,

to BrewDog beers has been epic and has shown just how many people share our frustration with the mainstream drink companies.

Some of the names of your beers are quite unique and sometimes downright weird. How do you come up with the imaginative names like Tactical Nuclear Penguin, Dead Pony Club, and Hello My Name is Ingrid?

It's definitely a team effort. We always try to think of something ballsy and irreverent—and most importantly we come up with names that no other brewery would use. Sometimes the names just come to us in a flash of inspiration, while other times it is a case of brainstorming over a tasting of a new beer.

BrewDog wins the award for most creative beer label for The End of History, which comes inside real stuffed squirrels and stoats. You also serve "Ghost Deer" from a mounted deer head. Who has the love of taxidermy?

I am the big taxidermy fan. Who doesn't love a little bit of macabre interior design? With

The End of History we had created this epic, game-changing beer, and we knew a simple glass bottle wasn't going to cut it. We needed a vehicle that was as wild as the beer itself. Those taxidermied critters are probably the most famous squirrels and stoats in the world!

Given how creative you both are with your brews, I can only imagine the shenanigans you have gotten into with your small batch home-brew. Was there an extreme batch of beer that you decided not to share or even drink because it was so outrageous?

We've had the odd brew go wrong, and obviously have created a lot of first batches that never saw the light of day. One of the first batches of Punk IPA we ever made was ruined after a glass thermometer broke in it, and I dropped my phone in the next one. This was at a time when we couldn't afford to waste a single drop so it was pretty catastrophic, but shit happens when you're brewing.

You had some obstacles in the early days, especially when the Portman Group (the trade organization of brewers and alcoholic beverage makers in the United Kingdom) accused you of breaching their code of practice. Can you take us through some the craziness that went on and how it made you feel?

The row with the Portman Group was crazy. They accused (but later cleared) us of promoting a bad attitude toward drinking with beers like Tokyo. But responsible drinking is at the core of what we do because we promote a better understanding of beer and alcohol and encourage people to think more about what they are drinking. Our beers are designed to be savored, not downed as quickly as possible before moving onto the next pint. I think they'd just never seen anything like BrewDog before, and didn't understand what we were trying to do. They backed down eventually. At the time we were still a tiny company, so the row actually helped us, as more and more people heard about us and we gained an army of new fans.

BrewDog is always challenging conventional thinking by creating over-the-top beers. I picture the two of you wearing wizards' robes

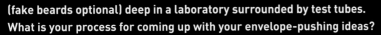

(fake beards optional) deep in a laboratory surrounded by test tubes. What is your process for coming up with your envelope-pushing ideas?

Ideas for new beers come from all over, but the key thing is to create something unlike anything else out there. From creating a beer at the bottom of the North Sea, to putting banned substances into a beer for the Olympics, we just want to push the boundaries of what beer can be. We also get many great suggestions from our army of craft beer fans, who are as passionate about beer as we are. We love hearing their weird and

wonderful ideas. Earlier this year we created #MashTag, a democratic beer where our social media community could vote on the style, ingredients and name.

How amazing is it to have not just one but ten BrewDog bars?

We actually have twelve bars now! We have eleven bars in the UK and one in Stockholm, and we have big plans to open more in the next few months including New Dehli, São Paolo and Berlin. Each bar is uniquely awesome

and has its own character, but each has the typical BrewDog atmosphere. A big part of what makes our bars so great is the amazing staff of beer nerds who are there to make sure every visit is epic.

In September 2013, the American television channel Esquire Network premiered Brew Dogs, a show where you and Martin travel across America visiting different American beer towns, celebrating distinctive craft beers and creating your own locally-inspired brews. The show is so fascinating; I love getting a glimpse into your lives and your brewing process. Now that you are celebrities, how does that affect your everyday lives?

The Esquire show was really cool to do, but we definitely don't see ourselves as celebrities! It was great to travel the States and meet some of our favorite brewers, create some insane beers and turn a few American drinkers on to craft beer. The series just finished in the States, so it's not really affected our lives in Scotland.

You two seem like great guys, why do you think there is so much animosity toward you from some in the beer industry?

I guess you could say we've had our fair share of scrapes over the years. From Diageo (a British multinational alcoholic beverages company) using dirty tactics to try and prevent us from winning an award, to the ASA (Advertising Standards Authority) complaint about our website content, to the Portman Group—we've definitely made our name known in a few camps. BrewDog stands for something innovative and different—we're not constrained by bureaucracy or profit margins, we are driven by passion to create awesome beers and we're having fun doing it. The reaction from big brands and tired institutions shows that they are out of touch. We've been critical of big drink brands, but our growth shows that there is a huge community of people who are as sick of mass-produced, soulless drinks as we are.

We can rest assured that BrewDog will continue to turn heads, not only with their way of doing business, but their marketing, their packaging and, of course, their beer. ●

Hell
Tallinn, Estonia

Inspired by Dan Brown's *Angels & Demons*, the design features an ambigramatic logotype, which also has a triple meaning: *gentle* in Estonian, *hell* in English and *light/pale* in German. ●

Pärnu Õlu
Pärnu, Estonia

Design by Brand Manual
Tallinn, Estonia
TheBrandManual.com

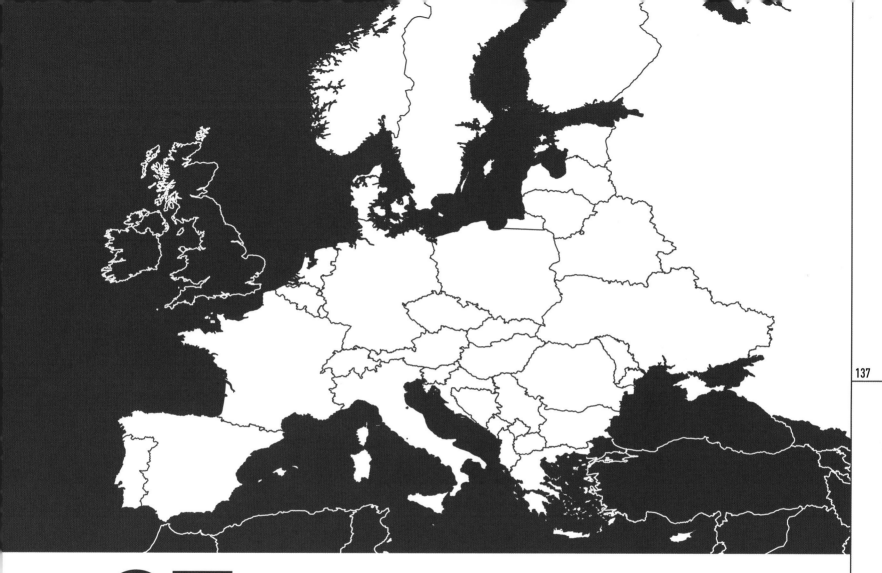

07 Europe

Mateo & Bernabé
Logroño, Spain
MateoyBernabe.com

Design by Moruba
Logroño, Spain
Moruba.es

2,5 ORIGINAL

Eine einfache grün-weiße Dose ! Keine teure goldene mit Prägung ! Nur eine simple Gestaltung ! Keine teure TV-Werbung ! Diese Ersparnis geht an Sie ! 2,5 Original Zutaten: 50% Bier (Wasser, Gerstenmalz, Hopfen) und 50% Zitronenlimonade (Wasser, Kohlensäure, Säuerungsmittel: Citronensäure, natürliches Aroma, Süßstoffe: Natriumcyclamat und Acesulfam K, Antioxidationsmittel: Askorbinsäure) ! Bezahlen Sie jetzt weniger für ein gutes *LEMON* ohne Schnörkel !

Bier-Mischgetränk
5,0 Biervertriebs-GmbH Postfach 13 37
38003 Braunschweig

5,0 ORIGINAL

Nur eine einfache rot-weiße Dose ! Keine goldene mit aufwendiger Prägung ! Nur eine simple Gestaltung ! Keine teure TV-Werbung ! Diese Ersparnis geht an Sie ! Wir haben so gut wie an allem gespart ! Außer an der Qualität des Bieres ! 5,0 Original ist ein Exportbier, gebraut nach dem deutschen Reinheitsgebot ! Zutaten: Wasser, Gerstenmalz und Hopfen ! Setzen Sie Ihr Geld besser ein ! Bezahlen Sie jetzt weniger für ein gutes *EXPORT* ohne Schnörkel !

5,0 Biervertriebs-GmbH Postfach 13 37
38003 Braunschweig

5,0 ORIGINAL

Nur eine einfache schwarz-weiße Dose ! Keine goldene mit aufwendiger Prägung ! Nur eine simple Gestaltung ! Keine teure TV-Werbung! Diese Ersparnis geht an Sie ! Wir haben so gut wie an allem gespart ! Außer an der Qualität des Bieres ! 5,0 Original ist ein Pilsbier, gebraut nach dem deutschen Reinheitsgebot ! Zutaten: Wasser, Gerstenmalz und Hopfen ! Setzen Sie Ihr Geld besser ein ! Bezahlen Sie jetzt weniger für ein gutes *PILS* ohne Schnörkel !

5,0 Biervertriebs-GmbH Postfach 13 37
38003 Braunschweig

5,0 ORIGINAL

Nur eine einfache orange-weiße Dose ! Keine goldene mit aufwendiger Prägung ! Nur eine simple Gestaltung ! Keine teure TV-Werbung ! Diese Ersparnis geht an Sie ! Wir haben so gut wie an allem gespart ! Außer an der Qualität des Bieres ! 5,0 Original ist ein Weizenbier, gebraut nach dem deutschen Reinheitsgebot ! Zutaten: Wasser, Weizenmalz, Gerstenmalz, Hopfen und Hefe ! Setzen Sie Ihr Geld besser ein ! Bezahlen Sie jetzt weniger für ein gutes *WEIZEN* ohne Schnörkel !

5,0 Biervertriebs-GmbH Postfach 13 37
38003 Braunschweig

5,0 Original - Feldschlösschen
Braunschweig, Germany
5-0-original.de

Design by feldmann+schultchen design studios
Hamburg, Germany
fsdesign.de

Maximus Pop-Up Store
Eindhoven, The Netherlands

The Maximus Brouwerij Pop-Up Store was created by graphic designer Leffe Goldstein for the 2012 Dutch Design Week. The store featured new package design for both of Maximus Brouwerij's beers: Brutus, a full-flavored American amber lager; and Stout 8, a rich, dark stout. In addition to the elegant bottle design, Goldstein also paid meticulous attention to the six-pack design. The inside of the carton has the map of the bike lane route from the Dom Tower, at the heart of Utrecht, to Maximus Brouwerij, located outside the city center. Along with the beers, the store also showcased Maximus plates, glasses and coasters.

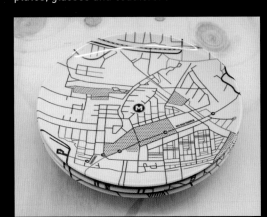

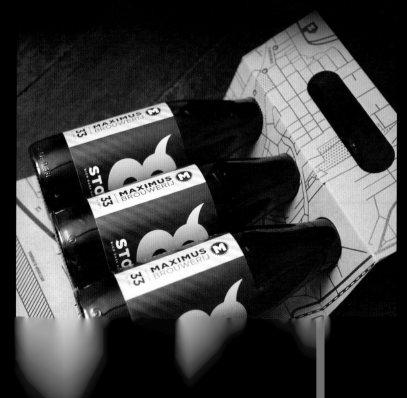

DIES IRÆ

TAG DES ZORNS
EXTREMES STARKBIER

Brauerei Gusswerk
Hof bei Salzburg, Austria
Brauhaus-Gusswerk.at

Design by Rolf Karner
Hof bei Salzburg
KarnerKreativ.com

Brouwerij Van Steenberge
Ertvelde, Belgium
VanSteenberge.com

Design by Geert Buntinx (BUG bvba)
Blaasveld, Belgium

Hell ★ Yeah
Lager Beer

Born in 1971 in Bonn, Germany, Dirk Behlau, also known as The Pixeleye, is not only an acclaimed graphic designer, but also a filmmaker and photographer. A self-taught artist, Behlau won his first award when he was 6 years old. After working in different agencies for years, in 1999 he went out on his own and started the Pixeleye Interactive studio. His impressive list of clients includes West Coast Choppers, Dickies, Burger King and Sony Playstation.

His unapologetically rock 'n' roll, hot-rod aesthetic gives all his work a very unique and distinct look and feel that has become his signature. "My

father was into rock 'n' roll music when I was a kid, so I listened to a lot of old records," Behlau says. "I've been into American cars my whole life, so things just came together. I love the lifestyle." His father was also a big fan of 1970s Italian Western films, so Behlau has been exposed to them since he was a kid, rounding out his early visual influences.

The Hell Yeah Beer project started when Dirk and his partner came up with the idea to create a rock 'n' roll beer without compromises. "Rough, raw with a FTW attitude." They were approached by Karlsberg (Karlsbräu), who decided to license the concept. Pixeleye Interactive was involved in

every aspect of the project. "The whole look of the brand and the beer itself is what I wanted it to look like," says Behlau.

For Behlau, beer and design have a lot in common. "Beer is a very passionate product. You can drink a special lifestyle you have chosen. I love to create products you can 'taste.'" In his opinion, good design has a very important place in the beer industry, especially in the world of small breweries. "Design is making a difference to the mainstream beers. Now there are even good-looking beers in that market. I love looking at all kinds of different beers from around the world in specialty stores. Every single one of them is telling a story, and good design evokes the wish to drink it. That's how it should be."

Karlsberg Brauerei GmbH
Homburg, Germany
HellYeahBeer.com

Design by Dirk Behlau / Pixeleye Interactive
Bonn, Germany
ThePixeleye.com

Kristjan Luiga
Tallinn, Estonia

Kristjan Luiga is an illustrator, designer and tattoo artist from the city of Tallinn, capital of Estonia. In December 2008, Luiga entered a competition to design a commemorative can for Estonia's biggest and oldest brewery, A. Le Coq brewery in Tartu. "I remember there was a very tight deadline. I think it was two weeks. At first I had no ideas, so I just drew the first thing that came into my head," says Luiga. His was one of three winning designs and Luiga was invited to attend the award ceremony, where he had the opportunity to meet Tarmo Noop, the president of A. Le Coq. From then on he worked directly with A. Le Coq's agency, Taevas Ogilvy, to finish the can design. The can sold in Estonia from April to December of 2009, and has since been featured in several design and illustration websites. ✍

A. Le Coq
Tartu, Estonia
ALeCoq.ee

Design and illustration by Kristjan Luiga
Tallinn, Estonia
Luix.com

Brewers & Union
Germany / Belgium
BrewersandUnion.com
Design by Brewers & Union

B1080 Beer
Battipaglia, Italy

Design by SUD Collective
Milan, Italy
sudcollective.it

Velkopopovicky Kozel (Efes Ukraine)
Kyiv, Ukraine
Kozel.ua

Design by Yurko Gutsulyak
Kyiv, Ukraine
Gstudio.com.ua

To Øl
Copenhagen, Denmark
To-Ol.dk

Design by Kasper Ledet
Copenhagen, Denmark
KasperLedet.dk

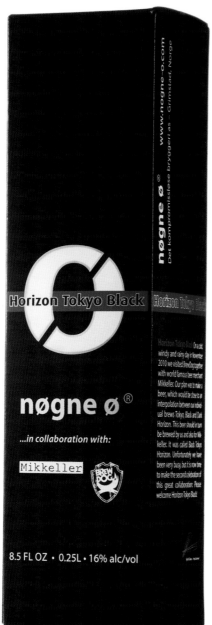

Nøgne Ø
Grimstad, Norway
Nogne-o.com

Design by Playcreate (Tor Jessen)
Oslo, Norway
Playcreate.no

Brauerei Gusswerk
Hof bei Salzburg, Austria
Brauhaus-Gusswerk.at

Design by Rolf Karner
Hof bei Salzburg
KarnerKreativ.com

Malteni
Wandignies-Hamage, France

Malteni's creators harness their region's rich traditions in cycling and beer. For professional cycling enthusiasts, the name of the 1960s and 70s Molteni team is legendary. Its leader, Belgian superstar Eddy "The Cannibal" Merckx, is the most prolific cyclist in history with over 520 races won, including five wins at Le Tour de France, five at Giro d'Italia, three at World Championships and an astounding thirty at single-day Classic races. It is fair to call Merckx the best cyclist of all time, and his Molteni team jersey is one of the most recognizable jerseys in the sport.

Most of the fame that Merckx and Molteni built was in the Northern France/Northern Belgium area where, even to this day, cycling races take place on cobbled streets normally reserved for cattle and farm vehicles. The effort and pain the cyclists endure during these races are epic and even considered legendary.

Malteni was born from the region's history and tradition in cycling and beer. The beer itself is hand brewed in collaboration with Belgian brewery Brasserie de Brunehaut in the heart of Wallonia, a region soaked in cycling and beer history. Malteni makes three different beers: Amber (Traditional Malteni Jersey), Wit (World Champion White Jersey), and Blonde (Tour de France winner's Yellow Jersey).

Malteni
Wandignies Hamage, France
MalteniBeer.com

Design by Malteni (Alexandre Voisine)
fr.linkedin.com/in/alexandrevoisine

AleBrowar
LĐbork, Poland
AleBrowar.pl

Design by Ostecx Créative
Poznan, Poland
Ostecx.com

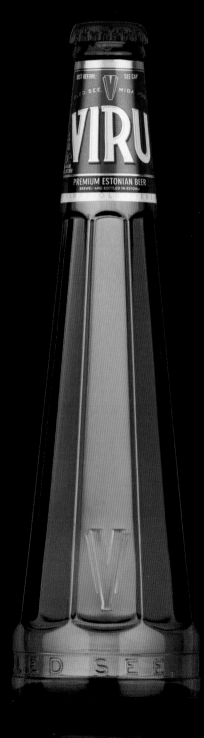

Viru Beer
Tartu, Estonia
ViruBeer.com

Design by Brand Manual
Tallinn, Estonia
TheBrandManual.com

To Øl
Copenhagen, Denmark
To-Ol.dk

Design by Kasper Ledet
Copenhagen, Denmark
KasperLedet.dk

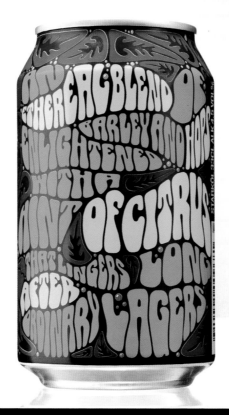

Brutal Brewing
Stockholm, Sweden
BrutalBrewing.se

**Design by Neumeister Strategic Design
(Lachlan Bullock)**
Stockholm, Sweden
Neumeister.se

2 X 8.5 FL OZ • 2 X 0.25L • 10% alc/vol

Nøgne Ø
Grimstad, Norway
nogne-o.com

Design by Playcreate (Tor Jessen)
Oslo, Norway
Playcreate.no

Minister (Ministerstwo Browaru)
Poznań, Poland
MinisterstwoBrowaru.pl

Design by Ostecx Créative
Poznań, Poland
Ostecx.com

Maximus Brouwerij
Utrecht, The Netherlands
BrouwerijMaximus.nl

Design by Leffe Goldstein
Utrecht, The Netherlands
behance.net/leffegoldstein

EUROPE

Liten
Ljus
Lager
Starköl
5,2vol%
33cl

Brouwerij Van Steenberge
Ertvelde, Belgium
VanSteenberge.com

Design by Geert Buntinx (BUG bvba)
Blaasveld, Belgium

Krönleins Bryggeri AB
Halmstad, Sweden
Krönleins.se

**Design by Amore
(Jörgen Olofsson & Håkan Schallinger)**
Stockholm, Sweden
Amore.se

Brauerei Kürzer
Düsseldorf-Altstadt, Germany
Brauerei-Kuerzer.de

Design by Gregorio Design
Düsseldorf, Germany
GregorioDesign.com

Mikkeller
Copenhagen, Denmark
Mikkeller.dk

Design by Keith Shore
Philadelphia, Pennsylvania
Photography by Robert Ureke

Birrificio Ex Fabrica (formerly La Fabbrica)
Grazzano Visconti, Italy
Exfabrica.com

Design by H-57 srl
Milano, Italy
h-57.com

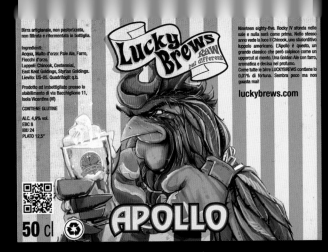

Birra artigianale, non pastorizzata, non filtrata e rifermentata in bottiglia.

Ingredienti:
Acqua, Malto d'orzo: Pale Ale, Farro, Fiocchi d'orzo.
Luppoli: Chinook, Centennial, East Kent Goldings, Styrian Goldings.
Lievito: US-05. Quadrifogli: q.b.

Prodotto ed imbottigliato presso lo stabilimento di via Bacchiglione 11, Isola Vicentina (VI)

CONTIENE GLUTINE

ALC. 4,5% vol.
EBC 8
IBU 24
PLATO 12,5°

Nineteen eighty-five. Rocky IV sfonda nelle sale e nulla sarà come prima. Nello stesso anno vede la luce il Chinook, uno sbalorditivo luppolo americano. L'Apollo è questo, un grande classico che però colpisce come un uppercut al mento. Una Golden Ale con farro, aromatica e decisa nel profumo.
Come tutte le birre LUCKYBREWS contiene lo 0,01% di fortuna. Sembra poco ma non guasta mai!

luckybrews.com

50 cl

APOLLO

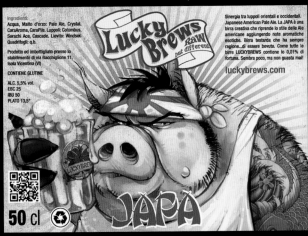

Ingredienti:
Acqua, Malto d'orzo: Pale Ale, Crystal, CaraAroma, CaraPils. Luppoli: Columbus, Sorachi Ace, Cascade. Lievito: Windsor. Quadrifogli: q.b.

Prodotto ed imbottigliato presso lo stabilimento di via Bacchiglione 11, Isola Vicentina (VI)

CONTIENE GLUTINE

ALC. 5,5% vol.
EBC 25
IBU 50
PLATO 13,5°

Sinergia tra luppoli orientali e occidentali. Japanese American Pale Ale. La JAPA è una birra creativa che riprende lo stile delle Ale americane aggiungendo note aromatiche esotiche. Birra testarda che ha sempre ragione...di essere bevuta. Come tutte le birre LUCKYBREWS contiene lo 0,01% di fortuna. Sembra poco, ma non guasta mai!

luckybrews.com

50 cl

JAPA

Ingredienti:
Acqua, Malto d'orzo: Pils, Caraaroma, Special B, Malto d'avena, Malto peated Chocolate, Carafa III. Luppoli: Summit, Styrian Goldings, Fuggles.
Lievito: Nottingham. Quadrifogli: q.b.

Prodotto ed imbottigliato presso lo stabilimento di via Bacchiglione 11, Isola Vicentina (VI)

CONTIENE GLUTINE
CONSERVARE IN LUOGO FRESCO

EBC 43
IBU 25

7,5% vol.

Anche i più duri hanno bisogno di passare l'inverno al caldo. Di rintanarsi a meditare sulle avventure passate per affrontare le prossime imprese.
La Winternest è una Scotch Ale per i più coriacei. Maltata, strutturata, leggermente affumicata e piacevolmente riscaldante.
Una calda copertina per i sensi, accompagnata da un tono torbato che rende placida la meditazione e agguerrito lo spirito.
Come tutte le birre LUCKYBREWS contiene lo 0,01% di fortuna. Sembra poco, ma non guasta mai!

luckybrews.com

Cerveza Artesanal SON
Córdoba, Spain
CervezaSon.com

Design by Jortober (Jorge Torrico Bernal)
Madrid, Spain
Jortober.tumblr.com

Illustration by Alfred Portátil
Córdoba, Spain
IlustracionesPortatiles.blogspot.com

Birrificio Ex Fabrica
Grazzano Visconti, Italy
Exfabrica.com

Design by H-57 srl
Milano, Italy
h-57.com

Mikkeller
Copenhagen, Denmark
Mikkeller.dk

Design by Keith Shore
Philadelphia, Pennsylvania
Photography by Robert Ureke

08 Asia & Oceania

Yeastie Boys
Wellington, New Zealand
YeastieBoys.co.nz

Design by Matt Gould
Auckland, New Zealand
MattGouldPortfolio.com

Gunnamatta design by Deflux Design
Christchurch, New Zealand
Deflux.co.nz

Black Heart Brewery
Melbourne, Australia
BlackHeartBrewery.com.au

Design by Amy Lewis Design
Melbourne, Australia
AmyLewisDesign.com.au

Photography by Lampoluce
Melbourne, Australia
Lampoluce.com.au

Hallertau
Riverhead, New Zealand
Hallertau.co.nz

Design by Degree Design
Auckland, New Zealand
DegreeDesign.co.nz

Fog City Original Artwork - Mimi Yoon

E9THBREWING.COM

Doss Blockos Original Artwork - Jak Rapmund

E9THBREWING.COM

East 9th Brewing
St Kilda, Australia
e9thbrewing.com

Design by Big Dog Creative
South Yarra, Australia
BigDog.com.au

Art by:
Jak Rapmund (Doss Blockos)
Mimi Yoon (Fog City)

ASIA & OCEANIA

Boundary Road Brewery
Auckland, New Zealand
brb.co.nz

Design by Barnes, Catmur & Friends
Auckland, New Zealand
BarnesCatmur.com

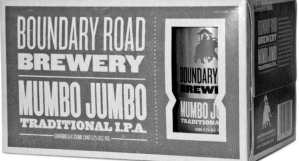

馨和 **KAGUA**

Blanc

馨和 **KAGUA**

Rouge

Nippon Craft Beer Inc.
Tokyo, Japan
NipponCraftBeer.com/kagua

Design by Mitsuyoshi Miyazaki
Tokyo, Japan
Mitsuyoshi-Miyazaki.com

8 Wired Brewing
Marlborough, New Zealand

8 Wired Brewing is the brainchild of Danish biochemist Søren Eriksen. The self-described "nomadic Danish brewer" decided to quit biochemistry and start 8 Wired in 2008 after he and his wife did a road trip through the United States. They stopped at every brewpub they passed. "That is when I decided that when we got back to New Zealand, I wanted to give pro-brewing a shot," says Eriksen. When asked how the craft beer scene in the United States compares to New Zealand, Eriksen says, "The U.S. is miles ahead of most countries when it comes to craft beer. I definitely see them remaining ahead in the foreseeable future. However, the world is getting smaller and smaller and the rest of the world is catching up fast. The reason why the U.S. would remain ahead is probably mainly due to the size of the country, combined with their interest in craft beer. With over 3,000 breweries (I have lost count but I think there are that many), other brewing nations will have a hard time catching up. Not that it is a race, of course."

The name of the brewery comes from No. 8 wire, a specific gauge of wire based on the British Standard Wire Gauge. No. 8 wire is supposed to be used for electric fencing, but in New Zealand its use is much more widespread than that. Kiwis have used it to fix just about anything. It's New Zealand's version of duct tape. "Over the years it has become a symbol of Kiwi ingenuity— their ability to fix any problem no matter how limited the resources," Eriksen says. "We think this fits our company pretty well: We don't have the resources or the abilities to run our own brewery, so we make do with what we have.

We also think that all our beers have a certain amount of ingenuity. Ingenuity in flavor, we like to call it."

Even with a strong tie to Kiwi culture, 8 Wired is proud to produce beer that isn't in the traditional New Zealand style. "Our beer is not old school Kiwi draught, Kiwi lager and Kiwi dark. In fact it is the exact opposite. Traditionally, these were the three styles brewed by New Zealand breweries. They were all pretty much the same beer with different color: lager was pale, draught was amber and dark was dark. Apart from a slight caramel flavor in draught and a slight roasted note in dark, they were all the same beer. Ten years ago, most of the microbreweries were still following this trend, which was a shame. Our beers were always meant to be much more challenging and creative than that."

Judging by the design of their labels, it's obvious that the beer is not the only thing that matters at 8 Wired. "There are so many different beers on the shelves these days, and it's important to look the part as well as taste good." To help them with that part of the business, they contacted Deflux Design in Christchurch. "Our original design was made by a local designer, Lisa Noble," says Eriksen. "However, she got too busy, so two or three years ago we started working with Deflux. I knew the guys from the craft beer scene, as they are passionate beer geeks. They started out designing our website and then carried on to do our labels as well. The process was very smooth. To some extent, they just carried on with the work Lisa had done, but they definitely also put their own spin on things. Usually I explain what we are brewing and what we envision for the label in terms of color and energy. Then they come up with a few designs and we roll with it from there." ●

8 Wired Brewing Ltd.
Marlborough, New Zealand
8wired.co.nz

Deflux Design
Christchurch, New Zealand
Deflux.co.nz

Founders Brewery
Nelson, New Zealand
FoundersBrewery.co.nz

Design by Barnes, Catmur & Friends
Auckland, New Zealand
BarnesCatmur.com

McLaren Vale Beer Company
McLaren Vale, Australia
MVbeer.com

Design by Parallax
Adelaide, Australia
ParallaxDesign.com.au

Kiuchi Brewery
Ibaraki, Japan
Kodawari.cc
Design by Kiuchi Brewery

Equator Design
Sydney, Australia

Equator Design in Sydney, Australia, started homebrewing a 5% pale ale to distribute to their clients and friends. The idea was to create a product that would make an impression and resonate with current and potential clients. "We decided to do just that with the labels. We debossed them to 'create an impression' on the thick stock through a local printing firm's letterpress machine," said Peter Bradley, studio manager and master brewer. The bottle cases are handcrafted out of native Australian wood.

Design by Equator Design (Mark Grey)
Sydney, Australia
Equator-Design.com

mike's Organic Brewery
Taranaki, New Zealand
organicbeer.co.nz

Design by TGM Design
New Plymouth, New Zealand
TGMdesign.co.nz

Hallertau
Riverhead, New Zealand
Hallertau.co.nz

Design by Degree Design
Auckland, New Zealand
DegreeDesign.co.nz

One Small Step IPA
Brewed and Designed by Josh Smith
London, UK
SkinnyWrists.co.uk

09 Home Brewers

Beer Farm
Brewed and Designed by Jim Dore
Overland Park, Kansas
JimDore.com

Brewbacca IPA
Brewed by Alex Heeton, Zara Hale and Sidekick Studios
Design by Katie Marcus
London, UK
WhatKatieDoes.net/portfolio

Garden Party IPA
Brewed by Josh Smith
Design by Katie Marcus
London, UK
WhatKatieDoes.net/portfolio

Gibson Brewing Co.
Brewed and Designed by Brian Gibson
Las Vegas, Nevada
GibsonBrewing.com
BrianDGibson.com

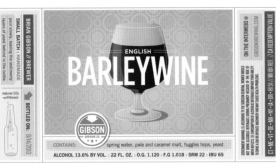

Henning's Hand Crafted Home Brew
Brewed and Designed by Matt Alvar
White Bear Lake, Minnesota
MattAlvar.com

Junction Brewing
Brewed and Designed by Matt Erickson
Menomonie, Wisconsin
MattEricksonDesign.com

Lucky Merlin
Brewed by John Logan Dunbar
Louisville, Kentucky

Design by Austin Dunbar
Cincinnati, Ohio
AustinDunbar.com

HOME BREWERS

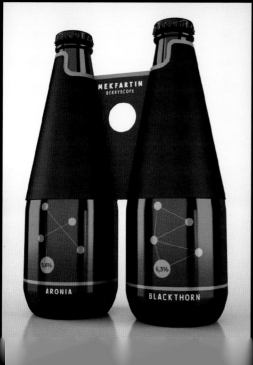

Martin Fek
Košice, Slovakia

Martin Fek started a home brewery under the name MEKFARTIN in 2010 in his native Košice, Slovakia. Martin, a design student at the Technical University of Košice, believes that the quality of what's inside the bottle is as important as what's outside. He takes great pride in the design of bottles. Each new batch of 25 or 35 liters (6.6-9.25 gal) gets a different package design.

WinterWit
4,8%

GreenJoy IPA
6,1%

SAHH

Traditional beer
7,9%

amy white mouse | **Objem**
Pivo kvasené pšeničné pivo | **0,33 l**
American wheat.
infúznym spôsobom. | **Alkohol**
voda, slady, chmel. | **4,6 %**
25. júna 2013

amy
white mouse
american wheat

Roscoe's Fine Ales
Brewed by James Dunseth
Portland, Oregon

Design by HUB Collective, Ltd. (David Zack Custer)
Portland, Oregon
HubLTD.com

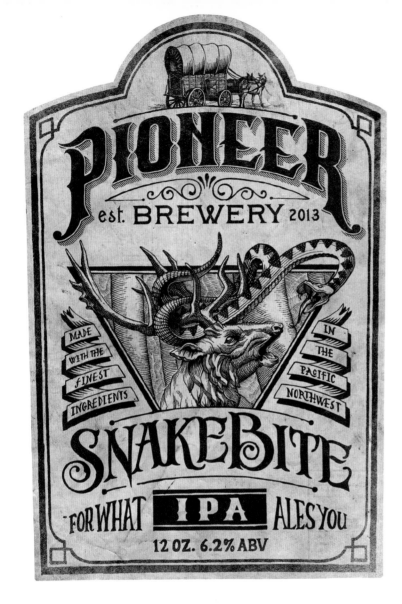

Brewed and Designed by Jason Thornton
Seabeck, Washington
behance.net/gallery/Pioneer-Brewery-Snakebite-IPA/10727019

ABV - 5.3%
IBU - 47

DEFTE Brew
New York, New York

Brewed and Design by DEFTE (Michael Delaporte)
Long Island City, New York
Defte.com

Photography by Kathryn Speeg
SweetPeaPic.com

Punk'n Brewster
Brewed by Josh Vandergrift
San Jose, California

Design by Martin Schmetzer
Stockholm, Sweden
MartinSchmetzer.com

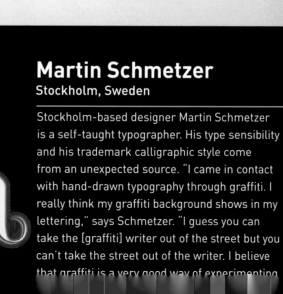

Martin Schmetzer
Stockholm, Sweden

Stockholm-based designer Martin Schmetzer is a self-taught typographer. His type sensibility and his trademark calligraphic style come from an unexpected source. "I came in contact with hand-drawn typography through graffiti. I really think my graffiti background shows in my lettering," says Schmetzer. "I guess you can take the [graffiti] writer out of the street but you can't take the street out of the writer. I believe that graffiti is a very good way of experimenting with the alphabet and to learn how the letters can come together. You don't have to follow any rules; you can just twist and bend the letters around until you've shaped them into something new and unique."

Schmetzer takes great care in his design from the very first step; the pencil sketch. "The sketching process is very important to me. I always start with pencil on paper before going

to the computer. I have tried drawing directly on the computer, but the design doesn't have the same flow, the same life. It looks forced."

Schmetzer applies his typographic eye to package design as a consumer and a professional. "I believe good design plays a role in every field. I often find myself picking items in the grocery store because of how the label reaches me. For me, the packaging is just as important as the taste."

Brewer Josh Vandergrift reached out to Schmetzer to collaborate on a label for Punk'n Brewster beer. "It was a pleasure working with Josh," says Schmetzer. "I had total freedom to try any style and composition. I don't believe we've had a single revision from my original sketch. We are both very pleased with the result."

Schmetzer, a beer lover at heart, thinks both of his passions come together well: "Good beer can be inspiring and can also help you clear your head." ✍

Fake Beer
Brewed and Designed by Klaus Bellon
Pittsburgh, Pennsylvania

Index by Brewery

Want to sample all the beers you've seen in this book? Of course you do! Here's a handy downloadable checklist to aid you in your efforts: CoolBeerLabelsBook.com/checklist

About the Authors

Daniel Bellon

Born in Bogotá, Colombia, of German descent, Daniel Bellon came to the United States at age seventeen. Already interested in typography and graphic design, Dan went on to be formally trained in graphic design at the University of Cincinnati's College of Design, Architecture, Art and Planning (DAAP). He has worked as a designer and art director for more than 15 years.

Dan inherited his love of beer from his father, a proud German, who showed him there's more to the beer world than the standard American ales available at the local convenience store.

Outside of design, typography and beer, Dan enjoys all things Star Wars, Mexican wrestling and 1970s Japanese robots. He loves watching professional cycling and Formula 1.

After twelve years as a New Yorker, Dan relocated to Pittsburgh to be closer to his family.

Steven Speeg

Steven was born in Ohio, and after living in Michigan and North Carolina, he settled in New England. He attended the Paier College of Art where he excelled at graphic design and discovered his affinity for typography and package design.

Today, Steven is an associate creative director with more than 13 years of professional experience.

In July 2011 Steven brewed his first batch of beer. Inspired by horror movies, he designed a logo and identity for his new, small batch home brewery: Spooky Brewery was born. All of his passions had collided: beer, design and 1980s horror films.

Speeg lives in Connecticut with his wife, three children and an overweight puggle. He is a proud member of the American Homebrewers Association and is currently on a quest to visit every brewery in New England.

On most weekends, he can be found in his backyard sporting a Halloween T-shirt, listening to Iron Maiden and brewing up a batch of hoppy ale.

DON'T MISS THESE OTHER GREAT TITLES
FROM PRINT BOOKS!

Lolita: *The Story of a Cover Girl*
BY JOHN BERTRAM AND YURI LEVING

What should Lolita look like? The question has dogged book-cover designers since 1955, when *Lolita* was first published in a plain green wrapper. The heroine of Vladimir Nabokov's classic novel has often been shown as a teenage seductress in heart-shaped glasses—a deceptive image that misreads the book but has seeped deep into our cultural life, from fashion to film.

Lolita: The Story of a Cover Girl reconsiders the cover of *Lolita*. Eighty renowned graphic designers and illustrators (including Paula Scher, Jessica Hische, Jessica Helfand, and Peter Mendelsund) offer their own takes on the book's jacket, while graphic design critics and Nabokov scholars survey more than a half a century of *Lolita* covers.

Graphic Content:
True Stories from Top Creatives
CURATED BY BRIAN SINGER

Graphic Content is a collection of true stories from a variety of creative contributors. Rather than promoting ideas like career advice for young designers, this book takes a turn in a completely different direction. It's filled with stories taken from real life experiences of over 50 creative people, and these stories are meant to provoke amazement, surprise, entertainment, and beyond. Read about an elevator meeting with Mick Jagger, slapping Catherine Keener in the face, organizing an impromptu board room presentation by John Belushi, a chance meeting with an astronaut, and much more. Each story is sure to evoke a different emotional response, but all are honest stories from real people meant to be shared with you.

Find these books and many others at **MyDesignShop.com** or your local bookstore.